Better Homes and Gardens.

365

pies & tarts

inspiring sweet slices for every day of the year

WILEY

John Wiley & Sons, Inc.

Library of Congress Cataloging-in-Publication Data

Better homes and gardens 365 pies and tarts.

    p. cm.

  Includes index.

  ISBN 978-1-118-21755-9 (cloth); 978-1-118-28097-3 (ebk); 978-1-118-28098-0 (ebk); 978-1-118-28099-7 (ebk)

  1. Pies. I. Better Homes and Gardens Books (Firm) II. Title: Better homes and gardens three hundred sixty-five pies and tarts.

  TX773.B4896 2012

  641.86′52—dc23

           2011051686

Printed in the United States of America

10 9 8 7 6 5 4 3 2 1

Meredith Corporation

Editor: Jan Miller

Contributing Editor: Amy Palanjian

Recipe Development and Testing: Better Homes and Gardens® Test Kitchen

John Wiley & Sons, Inc.

Publisher: Natalie Chapman

Associate Publisher: Jessica Goodman

Executive Editor: Anne Ficklen

Editor: Meaghan McDonnell

Production Editor: Maggie Vernon

Production Manager: Diana Cisek

Art Director: Tai Blanche

Interior Design and Layout: Holly Wittenberg

Manufacturing Manager: Tom Hyland

Our seal assures you that every recipe in *365 Pies & Tarts* has been tested in the Better Homes and Gardens® Test Kitchen. This means that each recipe is practical and reliable and meets our high standards of taste appeal. We guarantee your satisfaction with this book for as long as you own it.

Table of Contents

Pastry Primer

Once you've mastered a few basics, baking one of these yearned-for desserts is as easy as—well—pie!

The Art of the Pastry

USE EXACT MEASURES

Too much flour or water will make a crust tough, and too much shortening will make it crumbly. Also the water must be ice cold, to keep the shortening and butter from melting. Those bits of fat help separate the pastry into layers as it bakes—that's how your pastry gets flaky.

GO EASY ON THE FLOUR

Rolling the dough on top of a pastry cloth helps you avoid using excess flour, which can make a pastry tough. If desired, you can also cover your rolling pin with a cotton stockinette designed for pastry making; lightly flour both the cloth and the stockinette. When rolling the dough, work it as little as possible, because too much rolling also can make the pastry tough.

THE COVER-UP

To protect the crimped edge from overbrowning, fold a 12-inch square of foil into quarters. Cut off 3½ inches from the folded corners; unfold. There will be a 7-inch hole in the center. Loosely mold foil over edge of the pie before baking. Or use purchased pie shields to protect the crust.

Plates and Pans

Always use the size of pie plate or tart pan called for in a recipe. Here is the equipment you'll need.

PIE PLATES

These can be made of glass, ceramic, stoneware, aluminum, or tin.

TART PANS

The fluted sides of these pans make your tarts pretty; the removable bottoms make it easy to transfer tarts to serving plates.

Mastering Meringues

Follow these tips for airy, sweet meringues.

• Allow egg whites to stand at room temperature 30 minutes to bring more volume to the meringue.

• Use a large bowl made of copper, stainless steel, or glass, and make sure the bowls, beaters, and any other utensils are very clean and dry before using them. Oil or grease residue prevents whites from beating poorly. Also be sure no yolk gets into the whites when separating the eggs.

• Prevent shrinkage of baked meringue by beating egg whites until stiff peaks form (tips stand straight) and sealing the meringue to the crust's edge when spreading it over the filling.

• Prevent beading—small beads of moisture that can form on the surface of the baked meringue— by not overbaking the meringue.

• Prevent weeping—the water layer that can form between the meringue and filling—by spooning the meringue over the filling while it's still hot.

Pastry for a Single-Crust Pie

START TO FINISH **10 minutes**   MAKES **1 piecrust** (8 servings)

1½ cups all-purpose flour
½ teaspoon salt
¼ cup shortening
¼ cup butter, cut up,
  or shortening
¼ to ⅓ cup ice water

1 In a medium bowl stir together flour and salt. Using a pastry blender, cut in shortening and butter until pieces are pea size.

2 Sprinkle 1 tablespoon of the ice water over part of the flour mixture; gently toss with a fork. Push moistened pastry to the side of the bowl. Repeat moistening flour mixture, using 1 tablespoon of the water at a time, until all of the flour mixture is moistened. Gather flour mixture into a ball, kneading gently until it holds together.

3 Continue as directed in specific recipe.

NUTRITION FACTS PER SERVING:
191 cal., 12 g total fat (5 g sat. fat), 15 mg chol., 187 mg sodium, 18 g carb., 1 g dietary fiber, 0 g sugar, 2 g protein.

Pastry for a Double-Crust Pie

START TO FINISH **10 minutes**   MAKES **2 piecrusts** (8 servings)

2½ cups all-purpose flour
1 teaspoon salt
½ cup shortening
¼ cup butter, cut up,
  or shortening
½ to ⅔ cup ice water

1 In a large bowl stir together flour and salt. Using a pastry blender, cut in shortening and butter until pieces are pea size.

2 Sprinkle 1 tablespoon of the ice water over part of the flour mixture; gently toss with a fork. Push moistened pastry to the side of the bowl. Repeat moistening flour mixture, using 1 tablespoon of the water at a time, until all of the flour mixture is moistened. Gather flour mixture into a ball, kneading gently until it holds together. Divide pastry in half; form halves into balls.

3 Continue as directed in specific recipe.

NUTRITION FACTS PER SERVING:
303 cal., 18 g total fat (7 g sat. fat), 15 mg chol., 333 mg sodium, 30 g carb., 1 g dietary fiber, 0 g sugar, 4 g protein.

Cherry Almond Tart

PREP **45 minutes**   BAKE **35 minutes**   COOL **15 minutes**   OVEN **at 350°F**   MAKES **12 servings**

- 1 **recipe Nut Pastry**
- 2 **12-ounce jars cherry preserves**
- 1 **egg yolk, lightly beaten**
- 1 **teaspoon water**
- ¼ **cup sliced almonds**

1 Preheat oven to 350°F. Lightly grease a 13×4-inch rectangular tart pan or a 9- or 9½-inch round or square tart pan that has a removable bottom; set aside.

2 Prepare Nut Pastry. Press one pastry ball onto the bottom and up the sides of the prepared tart pan. Bake for 15 to 20 minutes or until pastry is light brown.

3 Meanwhile, roll remaining ball into a 13×10-inch oval. Using a fluted pastry wheel or pizza cutter, cut pastry crosswise into ¾- to 1-inch-wide strips.

4 Spread preserves over bottom of hot tart shell. Place half of the pastry strips on top of preserves ¾ inch apart. Give tart a quarter turn; arrange the remaining strips perpendicular to the first half of strips on filling. Press strip ends into edge of pastry.

5 In a small bowl combine egg yolk and the water; brush some of the mixture over pastry strips. Place tart on a baking sheet. Bake for 15 minutes. Remove from oven. Brush pastry strips with additional egg yolk mixture and sprinkle with almonds. Bake about 20 minutes more or until pastry is golden.

6 Cool on a wire rack for 15 minutes. Using a thin spatula or knife, gently loosen sides of pastry from pan; cool completely. Remove sides of tart pan.

Nut Pastry

In a large bowl stir together 2¼ cups all-purpose flour, ¼ cup ground toasted pecans or almonds, and 1 teaspoon salt. Using a pastry blender, cut in ½ cup shortening and ¼ cup butter, cut up, or shortening until pieces are pea size. Sprinkle 1 tablespoon ice water over part of the flour mixture; gently toss with a fork. Push moistened pastry to the side of the bowl. Repeat moistening flour mixture, using 1 tablespoon ice water at a time, until all of the flour mixture is moistened (½ to ⅔ cup ice water total). Gather flour mixture into a ball, kneading gently until it holds together. Divide pastry in half; form halves into balls.

NUTRITION FACTS PER SERVING:
381 cal., 15 g total fat (5 g sat. fat), 28 mg chol., 241 mg sodium, 58 g carb., 2 g dietary fiber, 28 g sugar, 4 g protein.

Cherry-Almond Creamy Cheese Pie

PREP 45 minutes BAKE 15 minutes COOL 30 minutes CHILL 4 to 24 hours OVEN at 450°F /350°F MAKES 10 servings

- ½ of a 15-ounce package (1 crust) rolled refrigerated unbaked piecrust
- 1 21-ounce can cherry pie filling
- ½ cup cherry preserves, seedless red raspberry preserves, or currant jelly
- ½ cup dried tart cherries
- 2 tablespoons lemon juice
- 3 tablespoons cornstarch
- 3 tablespoons cold water
- ½ teaspoon almond extract
- ¼ cup almond paste*
- ½ of an 8-ounce package cream cheese, softened
- 1 egg
- ¼ cup sugar
- 1 recipe Amaretto Whipped Cream
- ¼ cup sliced almonds, toasted

*tip

For best results, use an almond paste made without syrup or liquid glucose.

1 Let piecrust stand according to package directions. In a medium saucepan combine cherry pie filling, preserves, dried cherries, and lemon juice. In a small bowl combine cornstarch and the water; stir into cherry mixture. Cook and stir over medium heat until thickened and bubbly. Cook and stir for 2 minutes more. Remove from heat. Stir in ¼ teaspoon of the almond extract. Cover and set aside.

2 Preheat oven to 450°F. Unroll piecrust onto a lightly floured surface. Roll pastry from center to edges into a circle about 13 inches in diameter. Wrap pastry circle around the rolling pin. Unroll into a 10-inch pie plate. Ease pastry into pie plate without stretching it. Trim pastry to ½ inch beyond edge of pie plate. Fold under extra pastry even with the plate's edge. Crimp edge as desired. Do not prick pastry. Line pastry with a double thickness of foil. Bake for 8 minutes. Remove foil. Bake for 5 to 6 minutes more or until light brown. Remove from oven. Reduce oven temperature to 350°F.

3 Crumble almond paste into a medium bowl. Beat with an electric mixer on medium speed for 30 seconds. Add cream cheese; beat for 30 seconds more. Add egg, sugar, and the remaining ¼ teaspoon almond extract. Beat until combined, scraping sides of bowl occasionally. Carefully spread cream cheese mixture in pastry shell. Bake about 15 minutes or until set. Cool on a wire rack for 30 minutes.

4 Spread cherry mixture over cream cheese mixture. Cover and chill for 4 to 24 hours. Before serving, top pie with Amaretto Whipped Cream and sprinkle with almonds.

NUTRITION FACTS PER SERVING:
450 cal., 22 g total fat (11 g sat. fat), 70 mg chol., 153 mg sodium, 60 g carb., 2 g dietary fiber, 4 g protein.

Amaretto Whipped Cream

In a chilled medium bowl beat 1 cup whipping cream, 2 tablespoons sugar, and 2 tablespoons amaretto or ¼ teaspoon almond extract with an electric mixer on medium speed until soft peaks form (tips curl).

⏱ Cherry Crumble Pie Bars

2 cups all-purpose flour

1¼ cups ground almonds

¾ cup packed brown sugar

1 cup butter, cut up

¾ cup granulated sugar

1 tablespoon cornstarch

½ teaspoon finely shredded lemon peel

4 cups frozen unsweetened pitted tart red cherries, thawed and drained

½ teaspoon almond extract

1 Preheat oven to 350°F. Line a 13×9×2-inch baking pan with foil, extending the foil over edges of pan. Set pan aside.

2 For crust, in a large bowl stir together flour, almonds, and brown sugar. Using a pastry blender, cut in butter until mixture resembles fine crumbs. Remove 1½ cups of the mixture; set aside. Spread the remaining mixture in the prepared pan; press evenly onto bottom and sides. Bake for 15 minutes.

3 Meanwhile, in another large bowl combine granulated sugar, cornstarch, and lemon peel. Add cherries and almond extract; gently toss to coat. Spoon cherry mixture over hot crust, spreading evenly (mixture will be wet). Sprinkle with the reserved crumb mixture.

4 Bake about 40 minutes more or until top is golden and filling is bubbly. Invert onto a baking sheet; remove foil. Invert again onto a cutting board. Cut into bars.

NUTRITION FACTS PER SERVING:
148 cal., 7 g total fat (4 g sat. fat), 15 mg chol., 43 mg sodium, 19 g carb., 1 g dietary fiber, 2 g protein.

tip
Use your food processor to quickly grind your almonds, but stay close—if you let them go too long they could turn into almond butter.

Berries and Cherries

Cherry-Raspberry Pie

This recipe dates back to the 1960s, when two fruits were better than one.
This sweet-tart cherry-berry combination proves to still be a match made in heaven.

2   10-ounce packages frozen red raspberries in syrup, thawed

4   cups frozen pitted tart red cherries, thawed

1   cup granulated sugar

¼   cup cornstarch

½   teaspoon salt

1   recipe Pastry for a Double-Crust Pie (see recipe, page 5)

1   egg yolk, lightly beaten

1   tablespoon water

    Coarse sugar

1 Drain raspberries, reserving syrup. Drain cherries, reserving juice. Add enough of the reserved cherry juice to the reserved raspberry syrup to make 1 cup liquid; discard the remaining cherry juice. In a medium saucepan combine granulated sugar, cornstarch, and salt. Stir in the reserved syrup mixture and cherries. Cook and stir over medium heat until thickened and bubbly. Remove from heat; stir in raspberries. Cool for 30 minutes.

2 Meanwhile, preheat oven to 375°F. Prepare Pastry for a Double-Crust Pie. On a lightly floured surface, use your hands to slightly flatten one pastry ball. Roll pastry from center to edges into a circle about 12 inches in diameter. Wrap pastry circle around the rolling pin. Unroll into a 9-inch pie plate. Ease pastry into pie plate without stretching it. Trim pastry to 1 inch beyond edge of pie plate. Fold under extra pastry. Crimp edge high to keep filling from bubbling over. Do not prick pastry.

3 Roll remaining ball into a 12-inch-diameter circle. Using a 1- to 1½-inch star-shape cutter, cut stars from pastry circle. Transfer fruit mixture to pastry-lined pie plate. Arrange pastry stars on filling. In a small bowl combine egg yolk and the water. Carefully brush pastry stars with egg yolk mixture; sprinkle with coarse sugar. Cover edge of pie loosely with foil.

4 Bake for 25 minutes. Remove foil. Bake for 20 to 25 minutes more or until pastry is golden and edge of filling is bubbly. Serve slightly warm or cooled.

NUTRITION FACTS PER SERVING:
535 cal., 19 g total fat (7 g sat. fat), 41 mg chol., 481 mg sodium, 87 g carb., 5 g dietary fiber, 49 g sugar, 6 g protein.

Sour Cherry Pie

If you plan to make this recipe with fresh cherries, invest in a cherry pitter to make the pitting process easier.

PREP **40 minutes**   CHILL **2 hours**   BAKE **1 hour 20 minutes**   OVEN **at 375°F**   MAKES **8 servings**

- 2 **portions Sour Cream Pie Pastry or one 15-ounce package (2 crusts) rolled refrigerated unbaked piecrusts**
- 1½ **cups sugar**
- ½ **cup quick-cooking tapioca**
- ¼ **teaspoon salt**
- 1 **16-ounce package frozen unsweetened pitted tart red cherries or 4 cups fresh pitted tart red cherries**
- ¾ **cup dried cranberries or fresh cranberries**
- 1 **tablespoon lemon juice**
- ¼ **teaspoon almond extract**
- ¼ **teaspoon vanilla**
- 1 **egg, lightly beaten**
- 1 **tablespoon whipping cream**

1 If using, prepare Sour Cream Pie Pastry. Cover and chill as directed.

2 In a small bowl combine sugar, tapioca, and salt. In a large bowl combine cherries, cranberries, lemon juice, almond extract, and vanilla. Add sugar mixture to cherry mixture; gently toss to coat. If using frozen cherries, let mixture stand at room temperature for 20 minutes.

3 Meanwhile, preheat oven to 375°F. Line a baking sheet with foil; set aside. On a lightly floured surface, use your hands to slightly flatten one pastry ball. Roll pastry from center to edges into a circle about 12 inches in diameter. Wrap pastry circle around the rolling pin. Unroll pastry into a 9-inch pie plate. Ease pastry into pie plate without stretching it. (If using refrigerated piecrusts, follow package directions.)

4 Transfer cherry mixture to pastry-lined pie plate. Trim pastry even with pie plate rim. If desired, reserve pastry trimmings. Roll remaining ball into a 12-inch-diameter circle. Using a sharp knife, cut slits in pastry. Place pastry circle on filling; trim to ½ inch beyond edge of pie plate. If desired, reserve pastry trimmings. Fold top pastry edge under bottom pastry. Crimp edge as desired.

5 In a small bowl combine egg and cream. Brush top pastry with egg mixture. Roll the reserved pastry trimmings and cut out small shapes; place on pie. Brush cutouts with egg mixture. Place pie on the prepared baking sheet.

6 Bake for 1 hour and 20 minutes or until filling is bubbly. If pastry begins to brown too quickly, cover edge of pie loosely with foil. Cool on a wire rack.

Sour Cream Pie Pastry

In an extra-large bowl stir together 3¾ cups all-purpose flour, 1 tablespoon sugar, 1½ teaspoons kosher salt, and ½ teaspoon baking powder. Using a pastry blender, cut in 1¾ cups unsalted butter, cut up, until pieces are pea size. In a small bowl combine ⅔ cup ice water, 2 tablespoons sour cream, and 1 teaspoon vinegar. Add sour cream mixture all at once to flour mixture. Quickly stir to distribute; do not overmix. The dough should be slightly crumbly. Cover and chill for at least 2 hours or overnight. Divide pastry into three portions; form portions into balls. Use at once or wrap and chill for up to 3 days. Or freeze for up to 1 month; thaw overnight in the refrigerator before using.

NUTRITION FACTS PER SERVING:
652 cal., 29 g total fat (18 g sat. fat), 101 mg chol., 185 mg sodium, 94 g carb., 3 g dietary fiber, 52 g sugar, 6 g protein.

Cinnamon-Scented Cranberry-Almond Tart

To drizzle the white chocolate, simply hold a spoon about 6 to 8 inches above the pie and let thin strands drizzle over the surface.

PREP 35 minutes BAKE 25 minutes OVEN at 400°F/375°F MAKES 10 servings

- 1 **cup all-purpose flour**
- ⅓ **cup ground toasted almonds or hazelnuts (filberts)**
- ¼ **cup sugar**
- ¼ **teaspoon salt**
- ¼ **teaspoon ground cinnamon**
- ¼ **cup butter, cut up**
- 1 **egg, lightly beaten**
- 1 **tablespoon cold water (optional)**
- 1 **12-ounce package (3 cups) fresh or frozen cranberries**
- 1¼ **cups refrigerated raspberry juice or cranberry juice**
- ⅓ **cup water**
- 6 **inches stick cinnamon, broken**
- 1½ **cups sugar**
- 3 **tablespoons cornstarch**
- 1 **ounce white baking chocolate, chopped and melted**
- **Chopped toasted almonds**

1 Preheat oven to 400°F. For pastry, in a medium bowl stir together flour, ground almonds, ¼ cup sugar, salt, and ground cinnamon. Using a pastry blender, cut in butter until pieces are pea size. Gradually stir egg into flour mixture just until all of the flour mixture is moistened. If necessary, stir in the 1 tablespoon cold water, 1 teaspoon at a time, to moisten. Gather flour mixture into a ball, kneading gently until it holds together.

2 Press pastry evenly onto the bottom and up the sides of a 9- or 10-inch tart pan that has a removable bottom. Bake for 10 minutes. Remove from oven. Reduce oven temperature to 375°F.

3 Meanwhile, in a large saucepan combine cranberries, juice, the ⅓ cup water, and stick cinnamon. Cook and stir over medium heat until boiling. Boil gently, uncovered, for 3 to 5 minutes or until cranberries begin to pop. In a small bowl stir together 1½ cups sugar and cornstarch; stir into cranberry mixture. Cook and stir until thickened and bubbly. Remove and discard stick cinnamon.

4 Spread cranberry mixture over bottom of tart shell. Bake for 25 minutes. Cool on a wire rack. Remove side of tart pan. Drizzle tart with melted white chocolate and sprinkle with chopped almonds.

NUTRITION FACTS PER SERVING:
304 cal., 9 g total fat (4 g sat. fat), 35 mg chol., 118 mg sodium, 54 g carb., 2 g dietary fiber, 3 g protein.

⏱ Cranberry-Apricot Tart

If you don't have pumpkin pie spice on hand, simply stir together 1 teaspoon ground cinnamon, ½ teaspoon ground ginger, and ½ teaspoon ground nutmeg.

PREP **30 minutes**   BAKE **35 minutes**   OVEN **at 450°F/375°F**   MAKES **8 servings**

1   **15-ounce package (2 crusts) rolled refrigerated unbaked piecrusts**

½   **cup granulated sugar**

3   **tablespoons cornstarch**

1½   **teaspoons pumpkin pie spice**

¼   **teaspoon salt**

3   **15.25-ounce cans unpeeled apricot halves, drained and cut into quarters**

½   **cup dried cranberries**

1   **egg white, lightly beaten**

1   **tablespoon milk**

1   **tablespoon coarse sugar**

1 Preheat oven to 450°F. Let piecrusts stand according to package directions.

2 Line a 9-inch tart pan that has a removable bottom with one of the piecrusts. Press pastry into fluted sides of tart pan; trim edge. Do not prick pastry. Line pastry with a double thickness of foil. Bake for 8 minutes. Remove foil. Bake for 4 to 5 minutes more or until set and dry. Remove from oven. Reduce oven temperature to 375°F.

3 In a large bowl combine granulated sugar, cornstarch, pumpkin pie spice, and salt. Stir in apricots and cranberries. Spoon fruit mixture into tart shell.

4 Unroll the remaining piecrust on a lightly floured surface. Using 1- and 2-inch star- or other-shape cutters, cut out about 20 shapes. In a small bowl combine egg white and milk. Brush egg white mixture over pastry shapes; sprinkle with coarse sugar. Arrange pastry shapes on top of tart.

5 Bake for 35 to 40 minutes or until pastry is golden and filling is bubbly. Cool on a wire rack. Remove sides of tart pan.

NUTRITION FACTS PER SERVING:
413 cal., 13 g total fat (6 g sat. fat), 9 mg chol., 272 mg sodium, 73 g carb., 3 g dietary fiber, 2 g protein.

Cranberry-Cherry Pie ⏱

The cherries balance the taste of cranberries in this sweet tart pie.

PREP 30 minutes STAND 15 minutes BAKE 55 minutes OVEN at 375°F MAKES 8 servings

¾ **cup granulated sugar**

½ **cup packed brown sugar**

⅓ **cup cornstarch**

2 **tablespoons finely snipped crystallized ginger**

1 **teaspoon finely shredded orange peel**

4 **cups fresh pitted tart red cherries or one 16-ounce package frozen unsweetened pitted tart red cherries**

1 **cup fresh cranberries**

1 **recipe Pastry for a Double-Crust Pie (see recipe, page 5)**

Milk

Granulated sugar

1 **recipe Sweetened Whipped Cream (see recipe, page 31) or vanilla ice cream (optional)**

1 In a large bowl stir together ¾ cup granulated sugar, brown sugar, cornstarch, crystallized ginger, and orange peel. Add cherries and cranberries; gently toss to coat. Let fresh cherry mixture stand for 15 minutes, stirring occasionally. (If using frozen cherries, let mixture stand about 45 minutes or until cherries are partially thawed but still icy.)

2 Preheat oven to 375°F. Prepare Pastry for a Double-Crust Pie. On a lightly floured surface, use your hands to slightly flatten one pastry ball. Roll pastry from center to edges into a circle about 12 inches in diameter. Wrap pastry circle around the rolling pin. Unroll pastry into a 9-inch pie plate. Ease pastry into pie plate without stretching it. Transfer fruit mixture to pastry-lined pie plate. Trim pastry to ½ inch beyond edge of pie plate.

3 Roll remaining ball into a 12-inch-diameter circle and cut into ¾- to 1½-inch-wide strips. Weave strips over filling into a lattice pattern. Press strip ends into bottom pastry on rim. Fold bottom pastry over strip ends; seal and crimp edge. Brush pastry strips with milk; sprinkle with additional granulated sugar. Cover edge of pie loosely with foil.

4 Place pie on a baking sheet. Bake for 30 minutes (50 minutes for frozen cherries). Remove foil. Bake for 25 to 35 minutes more or until pastry is golden and filling is bubbly 2 inches from the edge. Cool on a wire rack. If desired, serve with Sweetened Whipped Cream.

NUTRITION FACTS PER SERVING:
481 cal., 17 g total fat (4 g sat. fat), 0 mg chol., 228 mg sodium, 79 g carb., 3 g dietary fiber, 43 g sugar, 5 g protein.

Cranberry-Pear Pie with Orange Cream

Avoid the white (bitter) part just below the orange peel when shredding it.

PREP **40 minutes** BAKE **1 hour** OVEN at **350°F** MAKES **8 to 10 servings**

- 1 **recipe Pastry for a Double-Crust Pie (see recipe, page 5)**
- ¾ **cup granulated sugar**
- ¼ **cup packed brown sugar**
- 3 **tablespoons all-purpose flour**
- 1 **teaspoon ground cinnamon**
- 1 **teaspoon finely shredded orange peel**
- ½ **teaspoon grated whole nutmeg or ¼ teaspoon ground nutmeg**
- ⅛ **teaspoon salt**
- 4 **cups sliced, peeled pears (4 medium)**
- 2 **cups fresh cranberries**
- 1 **tablespoon orange liqueur or orange juice**
  Milk (optional)
  Coarse sugar (optional)
- 1 **recipe Orange Cream**

1 Preheat oven to 350°F. Prepare Pastry for a Double-Crust Pie. On a lightly floured surface, use your hands to slightly flatten one pastry ball. Roll pastry from center to edges into a circle about 12 inches in diameter. Wrap pastry circle around the rolling pin. Unroll pastry into a 9-inch pie plate. Ease pastry into pie plate without stretching it.

2 In an extra-large bowl combine granulated sugar, brown sugar, flour, cinnamon, orange peel, nutmeg, and salt. Add pears, cranberries, and orange liqueur; gently toss to coat. Transfer pear mixture to pastry-lined pie plate. Trim pastry even with pie plate rim.

3 Roll remaining ball into a 12-inch-diameter circle. Using a 2-inch star-shape cutter, cut a star from center of pastry. Place pastry circle on filling; trim to ½ inch beyond edge of pie plate. Fold top pastry edge under bottom pastry. Crimp edge as desired. Using a sharp knife, cut slits in pastry around star cutout. If desired, brush top pastry with milk and sprinkle with coarse sugar.

4 Cover edge of pie loosely with foil. Place pie on middle oven rack. Line a baking sheet with foil; place on bottom rack to catch any drips. Bake for 40 minutes. Remove foil from pie. Bake for 20 to 25 minutes more or until pastry is golden and filling is bubbly. Cool on a wire rack.

5 To serve, top pie with Orange Cream.

Orange Cream

In a chilled medium bowl beat 1 cup whipping cream, ½ cup sour cream, 2 tablespoons powdered sugar, ½ teaspoon finely shredded orange peel, 1 tablespoon orange liqueur or orange juice, and ½ teaspoon vanilla with an electric mixer on medium to high speed until soft peaks form (tips curl). Makes about 2½ cups.

NUTRITION FACTS PER SERVING:
618 cal., 32 g total fat (17 g sat. fat), 78 mg chol., 435 mg sodium, 79 g carb., 5 g dietary fiber, 38 g sugar, 6 g protein.

Lattice-Top Cranberry Relish Pie

Filled with the flavors of fall, this makes for an excellent ending to a fall holiday (particularly the one with turkey!).

PREP 35 minutes BAKE 1 hour OVEN at 375°F MAKES 8 servings

½ cup dried cranberries

½ cup golden raisins

2 to 3 teaspoons finely shredded orange peel (set aside)

½ cup orange juice

1 12-ounce package (3 cups) fresh cranberries or frozen cranberries, thawed

1 cup sugar

¼ cup all-purpose flour

1 recipe Pastry for a Double-Crust Pie (see recipe, page 5)

1 egg, lightly beaten

1 tablespoon sugar

1 In a small saucepan combine dried cranberries, raisins, and orange juice. Bring to boiling over medium heat. Remove from heat; cover and let stand for 10 minutes. Transfer raisin mixture to a large bowl; stir in fresh or thawed, frozen cranberries, 1 cup sugar, flour, and orange peel.

2 Meanwhile, preheat oven to 375°F. Prepare Pastry for a Double-Crust Pie. On a lightly floured surface, use your hands to slightly flatten one pastry ball. Roll pastry from center to edges into a circle about 12 inches in diameter. Wrap pastry circle around the rolling pin. Unroll pastry into a 9-inch pie plate. Ease pastry into pie plate without stretching it. Transfer cranberry mixture to pastry-lined pie plate. Trim pastry to ½ inch beyond edge of pie plate.

3 Roll remaining ball into a 12-inch-diameter circle and cut into ½-inch-wide strips. Place half of the pastry strips on filling 1 inch apart. Give pie a quarter turn; arrange the remaining strips perpendicular to the first half of strips on filling. Press strip ends into bottom pastry on rim. Fold bottom pastry over strip ends; seal and crimp edge. Brush pastry strips with egg and sprinkle with 1 tablespoon sugar.

4 Cover edge of pie loosely with foil. Bake for 30 minutes. Remove foil. Bake for 30 to 35 minutes more or until pastry is golden and filling is bubbly. Transfer to a wire rack. Serve warm.

NUTRITION FACTS PER SERVING:
511 cal., 19 g total fat (7 g sat. fat), 42 mg chol., 344 mg sodium, 81 g carb., 4 g dietary fiber, 41 g sugar, 6 g protein.

⏱ Lemon-Cranberry Pie

While the combo of lemon and cranberries might sound like too much pucker for a pie, there's plenty of sugar to bring it into the perfect sweet-tart zone. Imagine how refreshing it will taste after a filling holiday meal.

PREP 25 minutes BAKE 55 minutes OVEN at 375°F MAKES 8 servings

1 recipe Pastry for a Double-Crust Pie (see recipe, page 5)

1¼ to 1⅓ cups granulated sugar

2 tablespoons all-purpose flour

1 12-ounce package (3 cups) fresh cranberries or frozen cranberries, thawed

2 lemons, peeled (with white membrane removed), halved lengthwise, and thinly sliced

1 egg white, lightly beaten

1 tablespoon water

1 tablespoon coarse sugar

1 Preheat oven to 375°F. Prepare Pastry for a Double-Crust Pie. On a lightly floured surface, use your hands to slightly flatten one pastry ball. Roll pastry from center to edges into a circle about 12 inches in diameter. Wrap pastry circle around the rolling pin. Unroll pastry into a 9-inch pie plate. Ease pastry into pie plate without stretching it.

2 In a large bowl combine granulated sugar and flour. Add cranberries and lemon slices; gently toss to coat. Transfer cranberry mixture to pastry-lined pie plate. Trim pastry to ½ inch beyond edge of pie plate.

3 Roll remaining ball into a 12-inch-diameter circle and cut into ½-inch-wide strips. Place half of the pastry strips on filling 1 inch apart. Give pie a quarter turn; arrange the remaining strips perpendicular to the first half of strips on filling. Press strip ends into bottom pastry on rim. Fold bottom pastry over strip ends; seal and crimp edge. In a small bowl combine egg white and the water. Brush pastry strips with egg white mixture; sprinkle with coarse sugar.

4 Cover edge of pie loosely with foil. Bake for 25 minutes. Remove foil. Bake for 30 to 35 minutes more or until the pastry is golden and filling is bubbly. Transfer to a wire rack. Serve warm or cooled.

NUTRITION FACTS PER SERVING:
411 cal., 18 g total fat (4 g sat. fat), 0 mg chol., 142 mg sodium, 61 g carb., 3 g dietary fiber, 26 g sugar, 4 g protein.

Fresh Strawberry Pie

Look for fresh, local strawberries in the spring to get some of the most flavorful berries around.

PREP 35 minutes · COOL 10 minutes CHILL 1 to 3 hours OVEN at 450°F MAKES 8 servings

- 1 **recipe Pastry for a Single-Crust Pie (see recipe, page 5)**
- 9 **cups fresh medium strawberries, stemmed and halved**
- ½ **cup water**
- ⅔ **cup sugar**
- 2 **tablespoons cornstarch**
- 1 **recipe Sweetened Whipped Cream (see recipe, page 31) (optional)**

1 Preheat oven to 450°F. Prepare Pastry for a Single-Crust Pie. On a lightly floured surface, use your hands to slightly flatten pastry. Roll pastry from center to edges into a circle about 12 inches in diameter. Wrap pastry circle around the rolling pin. Unroll into a 9-inch pie plate. Ease pastry into pie plate without stretching it. Trim pastry to ½ inch beyond edge of pie plate. Fold under extra pastry even with the plate's edge. Crimp edge as desired. Generously prick bottom and sides of pastry with a fork. Line pastry with a double thickness of foil. Bake for 8 minutes. Remove foil. Bake for 6 to 8 minutes more or until golden. Cool on a wire rack.

2 For glaze, in a blender or food processor combine 1½ cups of the strawberries and the water. Cover and blend or process until smooth. In a medium saucepan combine sugar and cornstarch; stir in pureed strawberries. Cook and stir over medium heat until mixture is thickened and bubbly. Cook and stir for 2 minutes more. Remove from heat; cool for 10 minutes without stirring.

3 In a large bowl combine the remaining 7½ cups strawberries and the glaze; gently toss to coat. Transfer glazed strawberries to pastry shell.

4 Chill pie for 1 to 3 hours. (After 3 hours, the bottom of the crust will begin to soften.) If desired, top with Sweetened Whipped Cream.

NUTRITION FACTS PER SERVING:
316 cal., 12 g total fat (5 g sat. fat), 15 mg chol., 189 mg sodium, 49 g carb., 4 g dietary fiber, 25 g sugar, 4 g protein.

⏱ Secret Strawberry-Rhubarb Pie

The pie uses almond cake-and-pastry filling to add a pleasing hint of nuttiness to the double-fruit filling.

PREP **30 minutes** BAKE **50 minutes** OVEN **at 375°F** MAKES **8 servings**

1 **recipe Pastry for a Double-Crust Pie (see recipe, page 5)**

⅔ **cup sugar**

¼ **cup cornstarch**

½ **teaspoon ground nutmeg**

¼ **teaspoon salt**

½ **of a 12-ounce can (about ½ cup) almond cake-and-pastry filling (not almond paste)**

1 **tablespoon lemon juice**

3 **cups fresh or frozen unsweetened sliced rhubarb**

2½ **cups sliced fresh strawberries**

1 **tablespoon butter, cut up**

1 **egg white, lightly beaten**

2 **tablespoons sliced almonds**

1 Preheat oven to 375°F. Prepare Pastry for a Double-Crust Pie. On a lightly floured surface, use your hands to slightly flatten one pastry ball. Roll pastry from center to edges into a circle about 12 inches in diameter. Wrap pastry circle around the rolling pin. Unroll pastry into a 9-inch pie plate. Ease pastry into pie plate without stretching it.

2 In a large bowl stir together sugar, cornstarch, nutmeg, and salt. Stir in almond filling and lemon juice. Add rhubarb and strawberries; gently toss to coat. (If using frozen rhubarb, let mixture stand about 30 minutes or until rhubarb is partially thawed but still icy.) Transfer fruit mixture to pastry-lined pie plate. Dot with butter. Trim pastry even with pie plate rim.

3 Roll remaining ball into a 12-inch-diameter circle. Using a sharp knife, cut slits in pastry. Place pastry circle on filling; trim to ½ inch beyond edge of pie plate. Fold top pastry edge under bottom pastry. Crimp edge as desired. Cover edge of pie loosely with foil.

4 Place pie on a baking sheet. Bake for 25 minutes (50 minutes for frozen rhubarb). Remove foil. Bake for 25 to 30 minutes more or until pastry is golden and filling is bubbly. Before the last 10 minutes of baking, quickly brush top with egg white; sprinkle with almonds. Cool on a wire rack.

NUTRITION FACTS PER SERVING:
461 cal., 22 g total fat (6 g sat. fat), 8 mg chol., 253 mg sodium, 62 g carb., 5 g dietary fiber, 5 g protein.

Strawberry Truffle Pie

This fresh strawberry pie has a base layer of white chocolate cream that makes it both surprising and special.

PREP 45 minutes CHILL 4 hours STAND 30 minutes OVEN at 450°F MAKES 8 servings

1 recipe Pastry for a Single-Crust Pie (see recipe, page 5)

3 ounces white baking chocolate, chopped

1 tablespoon butter

1 8-ounce package cream cheese, cubed and softened

2 tablespoons orange liqueur or orange juice

½ teaspoon finely shredded orange peel

¼ cup powdered sugar

1 cup whipping cream

1 pound fresh strawberries (about 2 cups), stemmed and halved

⅓ cup red currant jelly

Sliced kumquats (optional)

White chocolate curls (optional)

1 Preheat oven to 450°F. Prepare Pastry for a Single-Crust Pie. On a lightly floured surface, use your hands to slightly flatten pastry. Roll pastry from center to edges into a circle about 12 inches in diameter. Wrap pastry circle around the rolling pin. Unroll into a 9-inch pie plate. Ease pastry into pie plate without stretching it. Trim pastry to ½ inch beyond edge of pie plate. Fold under extra pastry even with the plate's edge. Crimp edge as desired. Generously prick bottom and sides of pastry with a fork. Line pastry with a double thickness of foil. Bake for 8 minutes. Remove foil. Bake for 6 to 8 minutes more or until golden. Cool on a wire rack.

2 In a small saucepan cook and stir chopped white chocolate and butter over medium-low heat until melted. Add cream cheese, liqueur, and orange peel; cook and stir until smooth. Remove from heat. Stir in powdered sugar. Cool to room temperature.

3 In a chilled medium bowl beat cream with an electric mixer on medium speed until soft peaks form (tips curl). Fold whipped cream into white chocolate mixture.

4 Spread white chocolate mixture in bottom of pastry shell. Arrange strawberries, stemmed ends down, on chocolate mixture. In a small microwave-safe bowl combine jelly and, if desired, kumquat slices. Microwave on 100-percent power (high) about 30 seconds or until jelly is melted. Brush strawberries with melted jelly and top with kumquat slices. Cover and chill for at least 4 hours.

5 Let stand at room temperature for 30 minutes before serving. If desired, garnish with white chocolate curls.

NUTRITION FACTS PER SERVING:
541 cal., 38 g total fat (21 g sat. fat), 93 mg chol., 313 mg sodium, 45 g carb., 2 g dietary fiber, 22 g sugar, 6 g protein.

⏱ Simple Raspberry Pie

Simple is such a lovely word, and so appropriate for fresh raspberries, which are at their flavorful best when barely adorned.

PREP **30 minutes** BAKE **1 hour** OVEN **at 375°F** MAKES **8 servings**

1 **recipe Pastry for a Double-Crust Pie** (see recipe, page 5)

1¼ **cups sugar**

⅓ **cup all-purpose flour or 3 tablespoons cornstarch**

5 **cups fresh or frozen red raspberries**

1 Preheat oven to 375°F. Prepare Pastry for a Double-Crust Pie. On a lightly floured surface, use your hands to slightly flatten one pastry ball. Roll pastry from center to edges into a circle about 12 inches in diameter. Wrap pastry circle around the rolling pin. Unroll pastry into a 9-inch pie plate. Ease pastry into pie plate without stretching it.

2 In a large bowl combine sugar and flour. Add raspberries; gently toss to coat. (If using frozen raspberries, let mixture stand about 45 minutes or until raspberries are partially thawed but still icy.) Transfer raspberry mixture to pastry-lined pie plate. Trim pastry even with pie plate rim.

3 Roll remaining ball into a 12-inch-diameter circle. Using a sharp knife, cut slits in pastry. Place pastry circle on filling; trim to ½ inch beyond edge of pie plate. Fold top pastry edge under bottom pastry. Crimp edge as desired.

4 Cover edge of pie loosely with foil. Place pie on middle oven rack. Line a baking sheet with foil; place on bottom rack to catch any drips. Bake for 30 minutes (50 minutes for frozen raspberries). Remove foil from pie. Bake for 30 to 45 minutes more or until pastry is golden and filling is bubbly. Cool on a wire rack.

NUTRITION FACTS PER SERVING:
484 cal., 19 g total fat (7 g sat. fat), 15 mg chol., 334 mg sodium, 74 g carb., 6 g dietary fiber, 35 g sugar, 6 g protein.

Juicy Raspberry Pie ⏱

Thick wedges of this crimson delight are sure to please the pie-lovers at your house.

PREP 30 minutes   BAKE 45 minutes   OVEN at 375°F   MAKES 8 servings

1   **15-ounce package (2 crusts) rolled refrigerated unbaked piecrusts**

4   **cups fresh or frozen raspberries**

¾   **to 1 cup sugar**

3   **tablespoons quick-cooking tapioca**

2   **tablespoons butter, melted**

1   **recipe Easy Vanilla Ice Cream (see recipe, page 8) (optional)**

1 Preheat oven to 375°F. Let piecrusts stand according to package directions. In a large bowl combine raspberries, sugar, tapioca, and melted butter; gently toss to coat. (If using frozen raspberries, let mixture stand for 15 to 30 minutes or until the fruit is partially thawed but still icy.)

2 Line a 9-inch pie plate with one of the piecrusts. Transfer raspberry mixture to pastry-lined pie plate. Trim pastry to ½ inch beyond edge of pie plate.

3 Unroll the remaining piecrust onto a lightly floured surface. Roll pastry into a 12-inch-diameter circle and cut into ½-inch-wide strips. Place half of the pastry strips on filling 1 inch apart. Give pie a quarter turn; arrange the remaining strips perpendicular to the first half of strips on filling. Press strip ends into bottom pastry on rim. Fold bottom pastry over strip ends; seal and crimp edge. Cover edge of pie loosely with foil.

4 Place pie on a baking sheet. Bake for 25 minutes (50 minutes for frozen berries). Remove foil. Bake for 20 to 25 minutes more or until pastry is golden and filling is bubbly. Cool on a wire rack. If desired, serve with Easy Vanilla Ice Cream.

NUTRITION FACTS PER SERVING:
259 cal., 5 g total fat (2 g sat. fat), 8 mg chol., 403 mg sodium, 51 g carb., 5 g dietary fiber, 26 g sugar, 6 g protein.

Raspberry Marzipan Tart

Marzipan is a sweet pliable mixture that consists mainly of ground almonds and sugar. This version also incorporates chopped pistachio nuts for an Italian twist.

PREP **40 minutes** BAKE **30 minutes** OVEN **at 350°F** MAKES **12 servings**

1 **recipe Rich Tart Pastry (see recipe, page 6)**

⅓ **cup seedless raspberry jam**

1 **recipe Pistachio Marzipan**

2 **ounces semisweet chocolate, cut up**

Chopped unsalted pistachio nuts (optional)

1 Preheat oven to 350°F. Prepare Rich Tart Pastry. On a lightly floured surface, use your hands to slightly flatten pastry. Roll pastry from center to edges into a circle about 13 inches in diameter. Wrap pastry circle around the rolling pin. Unroll into an 11-inch tart pan that has a removable bottom or a 10-inch pie plate or quiche dish. Ease pastry into pan without stretching it. Press pastry into fluted sides of tart pan; trim edge. Do not prick pastry. Line pastry with a double thickness of foil. Bake for 10 minutes. Remove foil. Bake for 8 to 10 minutes more or until pastry is golden. Remove from oven.

2 Spread jam over bottom of hot tart shell. Carefully spread Pistachio Marzipan over jam. Bake for 30 to 35 minutes or until filling is golden and firm when lightly touched. Cool on a wire rack.

3 In a small saucepan cook and stir chocolate over low heat until melted. Spread melted chocolate over marzipan. If desired, garnish with pistachio nuts. Chill tart until chocolate is set. Remove side of tart pan.

NUTRITION FACTS PER SERVING:
344 cal., 21 g total fat (10 g sat. fat), 105 mg chol., 143 mg sodium, 37 g carb., 2 g dietary fiber, 5 g protein.

Pistachio Marzipan

In a food processor or blender combine ⅔ cup sugar, ½ cup slivered almonds, and 3 tablespoons all-purpose flour. Cover and process or blend about 1 minute or until almonds are finely ground. Add ⅓ cup butter, cut up, and 1 egg; cover and process or blend until smooth. Add 1 additional egg, 1 teaspoon vanilla, and ½ teaspoon almond extract; cover and process or blend until smooth. Add ⅓ cup unsalted pistachio nuts, chopped. Cover and process or blend with several on-off pulses until combined.

Raspberry Pie with Chambord

The creamy, cream cheese topping on this pie makes it stand out from the crowd.

PREP 35 minutes BAKE 55 minutes OVEN at 375°F MAKES 8 servings

- 1 recipe Pastry for a Single-Crust Pie (see recipe, page 5)
- ¾ cup granulated sugar
- 3 tablespoons cornstarch
- 5 cups fresh or frozen red raspberries
- ¼ cup Chambord (black raspberry liqueur) or 2 tablespoons orange liqueur
- 1 3-ounce package cream cheese, softened
- ⅓ cup powdered sugar
- ½ teaspoon vanilla
  Dash salt
- ¾ cup whipping cream
  Fresh red raspberries (optional)

1. Preheat oven to 375°F. Prepare Pastry for a Single-Crust Pie. On a lightly floured surface, use your hands to slightly flatten pastry. Roll pastry from center to edges into a circle about 12 inches in diameter. Wrap pastry circle around the rolling pin. Unroll into a 9-inch pie plate. Ease pastry into pie plate without stretching it. Trim pastry to ½ inch beyond edge of pie plate. Fold under extra pastry even with the plate's edge. Crimp edge as desired. Do not prick pastry.

2. In a large bowl combine granulated sugar and cornstarch. Add 5 cups raspberries and Chambord; gently toss to coat. (If using frozen raspberries, let mixture stand about 45 minutes or until berries are partially thawed but still icy.) Transfer raspberry mixture to pastry-lined pie plate.

3. Cover edge of pie loosely with foil. Bake for 30 minutes (50 minutes for frozen berries). Remove foil. Bake for 25 to 30 minutes more or until pastry is golden and filling is bubbly nearly to the center. Cool on a wire rack.

4. Before serving, in a medium bowl beat cream cheese with an electric mixer on medium speed until smooth. Beat in powdered sugar, vanilla, and salt until combined; set aside. In a chilled medium bowl beat cream on medium speed until soft peaks form (tips curl). Fold about ⅓ cup of the whipped cream into cream cheese mixture to lighten. Fold in the remaining whipped cream.

5. Spread whipped cream mixture over top of pie. If desired, sprinkle with additional fresh raspberries.

NUTRITION FACTS PER SERVING:
474 cal., 24 g total fat (12 g sat. fat), 58 mg chol., 249 mg sodium, 57 g carb., 6 g dietary fiber, 3 g sugar, 5 g protein.

Roasted Peach Pies with Butterscotch Sauce

These pies are simply peaches baked in a biscuitlike crust—the only added sweetness comes from the butterscotch sauce. This recipe makes two 7-inch pies or one 9-inch pie.

PREP 40 minutes   CHILL 30 minutes to 2 days   BAKE 20 minutes   OVEN at 450°F/350°F   MAKES 6 to 8 servings

1	cup all-purpose flour
½	teaspoon baking powder
¼	teaspoon salt
¼	cup unsalted butter
½	cup sour cream
1	tablespoon milk
	Nonstick cooking spray
6	small or 4 medium peaches,* peeled and pitted
1	recipe Butterscotch Sauce
	Vanilla ice cream (optional)
	Fresh mint leaves (optional)
	Freshly ground nutmeg (optional)

1 In a large bowl combine flour, baking powder, and salt. Using a pastry blender, cut in butter until mixture resembles coarse cornmeal. Add sour cream and milk, stirring just until combined. Cover and chill for at least 30 minutes or up to 2 days.

2 Preheat oven to 450°F. For two 7-inch pies, divide dough in half. On a lightly floured surface, roll each half to a circle about 8½ inches in diameter. Transfer to two 7-inch pie pans. (For a 9-inch pie, do not divide dough; roll to a circle about 11 inches in diameter and transfer to a 9-inch pie plate). Trim crusts even with tops of pie pans. With a lightly floured fork, press sides of crusts into pie pans. Line each with a double thickness of foil that has been coated with cooking spray to prevent crusts from sticking. Bake for 8 minutes. Remove foil. Bake for 5 to 6 minutes more or until crust is golden. Cool on a wire rack. Reduce oven temperature to 350°F.

3 Cut peaches into thick slices. Arrange peaches in cooled crusts. Cover edges of pies loosely with foil.

4 Bake in the 350°F oven for 20 to 25 minutes or just until peaches are tender. Transfer to a wire rack. While pies are still warm, drizzle with ¼ cup of the Butterscotch Sauce. Serve immediately (crust becomes soggy as pie sits). If desired, serve with ice cream, garnish with mint, and/or sprinkle with nutmeg. Pass the remaining warm Butterscotch Sauce.

NUTRITION FACTS PER SERVING:
357 cal., 21 g total fat (13 g sat. fat), 56 mg chol., 142 mg sodium, 41 g carb., 2 g dietary fiber, 22 g sugar, 4 g protein.

*tip

If using the 9-inch pie plate option, you may need to add another peach.

Butterscotch Sauce

In a small saucepan melt ¼ cup unsalted butter over medium heat. Stir in ⅓ cup packed brown sugar and 1 tablespoon light-color corn syrup. Bring to boiling. Boil gently, uncovered, for 5 minutes, stirring frequently. Carefully stir in 2 tablespoons whipping cream. Cool for 5 minutes. Serve warm. Makes ½ cup.

Stone Fruits

Nectarine Cheesecake Tart ⏱

A little fruit, a touch of cheesecake, and a graham cracker crust make this a winning dessert.

PREP **25 minutes** BAKE **25 minutes** CHILL **2 to 12 hours** OVEN **at 350°F** MAKES **8 servings.**

1¼ **cups finely crushed graham crackers**

2 **teaspoons sugar**

½ **teaspoon ground cinnamon**

6 **tablespoons butter, melted**

12 **ounces cream cheese (one-and-a-half 8-ounce packages or four 3-ounce packages), softened**

⅓ **cup sugar**

2 **eggs**

½ **teaspoon vanilla**

2 **medium nectarines**

Finely shredded lime peel (optional)

1 Preheat oven to 350°F. Line a baking sheet with foil; set aside. For crust, in a medium bowl combine finely crushed graham crackers, 2 teaspoons sugar, and cinnamon. Drizzle with melted butter; toss gently to coat. Press mixture evenly onto bottom and up sides of a 9-inch tart pan that has a removable bottom; set aside.

2 For filling, in a large bowl combine cream cheese and ⅓ cup sugar. Beat with an electric mixer on medium speed until smooth. Add eggs and vanilla; beat just until combined. Finely chop one of the nectarines; stir into cream cheese mixture. Pour filling into crust-lined pan, spreading evenly.

3 Place tart pan on the prepared baking sheet. Bake for 25 to 30 minutes or until set in the center. Cool in pan on a wire rack. Cover and chill for at least 2 or up to 12 hours.

4 To serve, remove sides of pan. Slice the remaining nectarine; arrange slices on top of tart. If desired, garnish with lime peel.

NUTRITION FACTS PER SERVING:
353 cal., 26 g total fat (14 g sat. fat), 123 mg chol., 288 mg sodium, 26 g carb., 1 g dietary fiber, 14 g sugar, 6 g protein.

⏱ Nectarine-Pistachio Tart

Leaving the bright-color peels on the nectarines and sprinkling them with colorful green pistachios make this country-style dessert a brilliant feast for the eyes.

PREP **30 minutes**   BAKE **18 minutes**   OVEN at **375°F**   MAKES **8 to 10 servings**

1 recipe Pistachio Pastry
½ of an 8-ounce package cream cheese, softened
⅓ cup powdered sugar
⅓ cup whipping cream
2 cups thinly sliced nectarines or thinly sliced, peeled peaches (2 medium)
⅓ cup peach preserves or apricot preserves
1 tablespoon honey
2 tablespoons chopped pistachio nuts

1 Preheat oven to 375°F. Prepare Pistachio Pastry. On a lightly floured surface, use your hands to slightly flatten pastry. Roll pastry from center to edges into a circle about 12 inches in diameter. Wrap pastry circle around the rolling pin; unroll into a 10- to 11-inch tart pan that has a removable bottom. Ease pastry into pan without stretching it. Press pastry into fluted sides of tart pan; trim edge. Do not prick pastry. Line pastry with a double thickness of foil. Bake for 10 minutes. Remove foil. Bake for 8 to 10 minutes more or until golden. Cool on a wire rack.

2 For filling, in a medium bowl combine cream cheese and powdered sugar; beat with an electric mixer on medium speed until fluffy. Stir in 1 tablespoon of the whipping cream. In a chilled small bowl beat the remaining whipping cream until soft peaks form (tips curl). Fold whipped cream into cream cheese mixture. Spread filling into cooled tart shell. Arrange nectarine slices in a circular pattern on top of filling, overlapping slices slightly.

3 For glaze, in a small saucepan heat and stir peach preserves and honey over low heat just until melted. Press through a fine-mesh wire sieve; discard solids. Carefully brush or spoon glaze over nectarine slices. Sprinkle with chopped nuts. Serve immediately or chill for up to 1 hour before serving. To serve, remove sides of tart pan.

89

Pistachio Pastry

In a medium bowl stir together 1 cup all-purpose flour, ⅓ cup finely chopped pistachio nuts, and 2 tablespoons granulated sugar. Using a pastry blender, cut in ⅓ cup butter, cut up, until pieces are pea size. Sprinkle 1 tablespoon ice water over part of the flour mixture; gently toss with a fork. Push moistened pastry to the side of the bowl. Repeat moistening flour mixture, using 1 tablespoon ice water at a time, until all of the flour mixture is moistened (3 to 5 tablespoons ice water total). Gather flour mixture into a ball, kneading gently until it holds together. If necessary, wrap dough in plastic wrap and chill for 30 to 60 minutes or until dough is easy to handle.

NUTRITION FACTS PER SERVING:
335 cal., 20 g total fat (11 g sat. fat), 50 mg chol., 126 mg sodium, 36 g carb., 2 g dietary fiber, 5 g protein.

Brandy Plum Pie

PREP 40 minutes BAKE 45 minutes OVEN at 375°F MAKES 8 servings

1 recipe Pastry for a Single-Crust Pie (see recipe, page 5)

1 recipe Crumb Topping

¾ cup packed brown sugar

¼ cup all-purpose flour

¼ cup brandy or apple juice

⅛ teaspoon ground nutmeg (optional)

4 cups sliced plums (about 1¾ pounds)

⅓ cup chopped almonds or pecans

1 Preheat oven to 375°F. Prepare Pastry for a Single-Crust Pie. On a lightly floured surface, use your hands to slightly flatten pastry. Roll pastry from center to edges into a circle about 12 inches in diameter. Wrap pastry circle around the rolling pin. Unroll into a 9-inch pie plate. Ease pastry into pie plate without stretching it. Trim pastry to ½ inch beyond edge of pie plate. Fold under extra pastry even with the plate's edge. Crimp edge as desired. Do not prick pastry. Prepare Crumb Topping; set aside.

2 In a large bowl stir together brown sugar, flour, brandy, and, if desired, nutmeg. Add plums; gently toss to coat. Transfer plum mixture to the pastry-lined pie plate. Sprinkle Crumb Topping over plum mixture. Sprinkle with chopped nuts.

3 Cover edge of pie loosely with foil. Bake for 25 minutes. Remove foil. Bake for 20 to 25 minutes more or until top is golden. Cool on a wire rack.

NUTRITION FACTS PER SERVING: *464 cal., 20 g total fat (6 g sat. fat), 15 mg chol., 147 mg sodium, 65 g carb., 2 g dietary fiber, 5 g protein.*

Crumb Topping

In a medium bowl stir together ½ cup all-purpose flour and ½ cup packed brown sugar. Using a pastry blender, cut in 3 tablespoons butter until mixture resembles coarse crumbs.

Plum Frangipane Tart

Frangipane [FRAN-juh-payn] is a pastry made with flour, butter, egg, and almond paste. It is similar in texture to cream puff pastry, and its tender, barely sweet taste highlights plums at their peak of flavor.

PREP **40 minutes** CHILL **30 minutes** BAKE **1 hour** COOL **1 hour 30 minutes** OVEN **at 375°F** MAKES **8 servings**

- 1 **cup all-purpose flour**
- 3 **tablespoons sugar**
- **Dash salt**
- 6 **tablespoons butter, cut up**
- 1 **egg yolk**
- 1 **tablespoon water**
- ¼ **cup almond paste, crumbled**
- 2 **tablespoons butter, softened**
- ¼ **cup sugar**
- 1 **egg white**
- 1 **tablespoon all-purpose flour**
- 1 **teaspoon finely shredded orange peel**
- 1 **teaspoon vanilla**
- ¼ **teaspoon salt**
- 12 **ounces ripe plums, pitted and each cut into eighths**
- 1 **tablespoon sugar**
- 2 **tablespoons peach preserves, melted**

1 In a food processor combine 1 cup flour, 3 tablespoons sugar, and the dash salt; cover and process until combined. Add 6 tablespoons butter and process until crumbly. Add egg yolk and water; process just until mixture holds together. Cover and chill for 30 minutes.

2 Preheat oven to 375°F. Place a floured sheet of waxed paper on work surface; turn dough out onto waxed paper. Flour another sheet of waxed paper and place over dough, floured side down. Roll pastry from center to edges into a circle about 11 inches in diameter. Remove top piece of waxed paper. Invert pastry and ease into 9½-inch tart pan that has a removable bottom, removing the remaining waxed paper. Press pastry into fluted sides of tart pan; trim edge. Place tart shell in freezer until ready to use.

3 For filling, in a food processor combine almond paste and the 2 tablespoons butter; cover and process until smooth. Add ¼ cup sugar, egg white, 1 tablespoon flour, orange peel, vanilla, and ¼ teaspoon salt. Cover and process until creamy. Spoon filling into the tart shell. Top with plums. Sprinkle with the 1 tablespoon sugar.

4 Bake for 45 minutes. Cover loosely with foil. Bake about 15 minutes more or until filling is set and plums are tender. Remove foil. Brush melted preserves over warm tart. To serve, remove sides of tart pan. Cool on a wire rack for 1½ hours. Cover and chill within 2 hours.

NUTRITION FACTS PER SERVING:
Ed: Nutrition info was missing in ms file.

Raisin Plum Pie

Sweet, chewy raisins plump as they bake and balance the tangy-tart flavors of cranberries and plums.

PREP **40 minutes** BAKE **50 minutes** OVEN at **375°F** MAKES **8 servings**

1 recipe Whole Wheat Pastry
¾ cup packed brown sugar
2 tablespoons all-purpose flour
5 to 6 plums (about 1 pound), pitted and cut into bite-size pieces (2 cups)
½ cup raisins
½ cup dried currants
½ cup fresh or frozen cranberries
2 tablespoons butter, cut up
Milk
Granulated sugar

1 Preheat oven to 375°F. Prepare Whole Wheat Pastry. On a lightly floured surface, use your hands to slightly flatten one pastry ball. Roll pastry from center to edges into a circle about 12 inches in diameter. Wrap pastry circle around the rolling pin. Unroll pastry into a 9-inch pie plate. Ease pastry into pie plate without stretching it.

2 For filling, in large bowl combine brown sugar and flour. Add plums, raisins, currants, and cranberries; toss to coat. Transfer filling to pastry-lined pie plate. Trim pastry to ½ inch beyond edge of pie plate. Dot filling with butter.

3 Roll remaining pastry into a 10- to 12-inch-diameter circle; cut into ½-inch-wide strips. Weave strips over filling into a lattice pattern. Press strip ends into bottom pastry on rim. Fold bottom pastry over strip ends; seal and crimp edge.

4 Brush top with milk; sprinkle with granulated sugar. Cover edge of pie loosely with foil. Bake for 25 minutes. Remove foil. Bake for 25 to 30 minutes more or until filling is bubbly and pastry is golden. Cool on a wire rack.

NUTRITION FACTS PER SERVING:
479 cal., 20 g total fat (6 g sat. fat), 8 mg chol., 175 mg sodium, 72 g carb., 5 g dietary fiber, 38 g sugar, 6 g protein.

Whole Wheat Pastry

In a large bowl stir together 1½ cups all-purpose flour, 1 cup whole wheat flour, and ½ teaspoon salt. Using a pastry blender, cut in ⅔ cup shortening until pieces are pea size. Sprinkle 1 tablespoon cold water over part of the flour mixture; gently toss with a fork. Push moistened pastry to the side of the bowl. Repeat moistening flour mixture, using 1 tablespoon cold water at a time, until all of the flour mixture is moistened (7 to 9 tablespoons cold water total). Gather flour mixture into a ball, kneading gently until it holds together. Divide pastry in half; form halves into balls.

Extreme Chocolate Pie

Most chocolate lovers agree that if one chocolate is good, two are better. With that in mind, an ultra-rich brownie crust is added to a much-loved French silk chocolate pie.

PREP 35 minutes BAKE 20 minutes CHILL 4 to 24 hours OVEN at 350°F MAKES 10 servings

1 8-ounce package brownie mix

1 cup sugar

¾ cup butter, softened

6 ounces unsweetened chocolate, melted and cooled

1 teaspoon vanilla

¾ cup refrigerated or frozen egg product, thawed

1 recipe Sweetened Whipped Cream (see recipe, page 31)

1 1.45-ounce bar dark sweet chocolate, shaved or coarsely chopped

1 Preheat oven to 350°F. Grease a 9-inch pie plate; set aside. Prepare brownie mix according to package directions. Spread batter in the prepared pie plate. Bake for 20 to 25 minutes or until a toothpick inserted in the center comes out clean. Cool on a wire rack.

2 For filling, in a medium bowl beat sugar and butter with an electric mixer on medium speed about 4 minutes or until light and fluffy. Stir in melted chocolate and vanilla. Gradually add egg product, beating on low speed until combined. Beat on medium to high speed about 1 minute or until light and fluffy, scraping sides of bowl frequently.

3 Spread filling over baked brownie layer. Cover and chill for 4 to 24 hours. To serve, top with Sweetened Whipped Cream and sprinkle with shaved chocolate.

NUTRITION FACTS PER SERVING:
514 cal., 36 g total fat (21 g sat. fat), 91 mg chol., 250 mg sodium, 50 g carb., 3 g dietary fiber, 37 g sugar, 6 g protein.

Fudgy Caramel and Peanut Butter-Brownie Pie

PREP **35 minutes** BAKE **50 minutes** OVEN **at 450°F/325°F** MAKES **10 servings**

- 1 **recipe Pastry for a Single-Crust Pie (see recipe, page 5)**
- 1 **cup caramel baking bits**
- 3 **ounces bittersweet chocolate, chopped**
- 3 **tablespoons butter**
- 3 **tablespoons creamy peanut butter**
- 4 **eggs, lightly beaten**
- 1 **cup packed brown sugar**
- ¼ **cup all-purpose flour**
- 2 **tablespoons whipping cream**
- 1 **tablespoon coffee liqueur, chocolate liqueur, or whipping cream**
- 1 **tablespoon vanilla**
- ½ **teaspoon salt**
- 1 **cup honey-roasted peanuts**
- 1 **recipe Easy Vanilla Ice Cream (see recipe, page 8) (optional)**

1 Preheat oven to 450°F. Prepare Pastry for a Single-Crust Pie. On a lightly floured surface, use your hands to slightly flatten pastry. Roll pastry from center to edges into a circle about 12 inches in diameter. Wrap pastry circle around the rolling pin. Unroll into a 9-inch pie plate. Ease pastry into pie plate without stretching it. Trim pastry to ½ inch beyond edge of pie plate. Fold under extra pastry even with the plate's edge. Crimp edge as desired. Do not prick pastry. Line pastry with a double thickness of foil. Bake for 8 minutes. Remove foil. Bake for 6 to 8 minutes more or until golden. Cool on a wire rack. Reduce oven temperature to 325°F.

2 Sprinkle caramel bits onto bottom of pastry shell. In a small saucepan cook and stir chocolate, butter, and peanut butter over medium-low heat until melted and smooth. Remove from heat.

3 In a large bowl whisk together eggs, brown sugar, flour, cream, liqueur, vanilla, and salt. Add chocolate mixture; whisk just until combined. Stir in peanuts. Pour mixture over caramel bits.

4 Cover edge of pie loosely with foil. Bake in the 325°F oven for 30 minutes. Remove foil. Bake for 20 to 25 minutes more or until filling appears set in center. Cool on a wire rack. If desired, serve with Easy Vanilla Ice Cream.

NUTRITION FACTS PER SERVING:
489 cal., 25 g total fat (9 g sat. fat), 98 mg chol., 344 mg sodium, 59 g carb., 2 g dietary fiber, 40 g sugar, 9 g protein.

Ganache-Glazed Peanut Butter Tart

PREP 30 minutes BAKE 10 minutes CHILL 4 to 24 hours COOL 10 minutes STAND 10 minutes OVEN at 350°F

MAKES 16 servings

- 1 cup crushed chocolate wafer cookies
- 3 tablespoons sugar
- 3 tablespoons butter, melted
- 1½ cups half-and-half or light cream
- 2 tablespoons all-purpose flour
- ¼ teaspoon salt
- 3 egg yolks
- ⅓ cup sugar
- ½ cup creamy peanut butter
- 1 teaspoon vanilla
- 4 ounces bittersweet chocolate, chopped
- 5 tablespoons butter, cut up
- 1 tablespoon light-color corn syrup

1 Preheat oven to 350°F. For crust, in a medium bowl combine crushed chocolate cookies and 3 tablespoons sugar. Drizzle with melted butter; toss to combine. Spread crumb mixture in a 9-inch tart pan that has a removable bottom; press onto bottom and sides. Bake about 10 minutes or until set. Cool on a wire rack.

2 For filling, in a medium saucepan combine half-and-half, flour, and salt. Cook over medium heat until simmering, stirring frequently. In a small bowl combine egg yolks and ⅓ cup sugar. Gradually stir about half of the hot mixture into egg yolk mixture. Return egg yolk mixture to saucepan. Cook and stir over medium heat until thickened and bubbly. Remove from heat. Whisk in peanut butter and vanilla until combined. Pour filling into crust, spreading evenly. Cover and chill for 3 hours.

3 For ganache, in a small saucepan combine chocolate and 5 tablespoons butter. Cook and stir over low heat until melted. Remove from heat. Stir in corn syrup; cool for 10 minutes.

4 Pour ganache over filling, tilting pan to allow ganache to flow evenly over tart. Cover and chill for 1 to 24 hours.

5 Let stand at room temperature for 10 minutes before serving. Using a thin spatula or knife, gently loosen sides of crust from pan. Remove side of tart pan. To cut, dip a sharp knife into hot water; dry knife. Quickly score top of the tart with warm knife. Cut tart along score marks.

NUTRITION FACTS PER SERVING:
235 cal., 17 g total fat (8 g sat. fat), 63 mg chol., 166 mg sodium, 19 g carb., 1 g dietary fiber, 12 g sugar, 4 g protein.

White Chocolate-Macadamia Brownie Pie

The white chocolate sauce would be a delicious topping for regular brownies the next time you make them.

PREP **30 minutes** BAKE **50 minutes** OVEN at **350°F** MAKES **12 servings**

1   **recipe Pastry for a Single-Crust Pie (see recipe, page 5)**

1   **cup all-purpose flour**

3   **ounces white baking chocolate with cocoa butter, grated**

¼   **teaspoon baking powder**

3   **eggs, lightly beaten**

¾   **cup sugar**

¼   **cup unsalted butter, melted and cooled**

1   **teaspoon vanilla**

1   **cup chopped macadamia nuts, pecans, or almonds, toasted**

3   **ounces white baking chocolate with cocoa butter, chopped**

Chocolate ice cream (optional)

1   **recipe White Chocolate Sauce (optional)**

1 Preheat oven to 350°F. Prepare Pastry for a Single-Crust Pie. On a lightly floured surface, use your hands to slightly flatten pastry. Roll pastry from center to edges into a circle about 12 inches in diameter. Wrap pastry circle around the rolling pin. Unroll into a 9-inch pie plate. Ease pastry into pie plate without stretching it. Trim pastry to ½ inch beyond edge of pie plate. Fold under extra pastry even with the plate's edge. Crimp edge as desired. Do not prick pastry.

2 For filling, in a small bowl combine flour, 3 ounces grated white chocolate, and baking powder; set aside. In a medium bowl stir together eggs, sugar, melted butter, and vanilla just until combined. Stir in flour mixture, nuts, and 3 ounces chopped white chocolate. Spread filling in pastry-lined pie plate.

3 Bake for 50 to 55 minutes or until a toothpick inserted near the center comes out clean. Transfer to a wire rack. Serve slightly warm or cooled. If desired, serve with ice cream and White Chocolate Sauce.

NUTRITION FACTS PER SERVING:
Ed: Nutrition info was missing in ms file.

White Chocolate Sauce

In a small heavy saucepan bring ⅔ cup whipping cream and 1 teaspoon vanilla just to boiling, stirring frequently. Remove from heat. In a small bowl combine 1 egg yolk, ⅓ cup sugar, and 2 to 4 tablespoons of the hot mixture. Beat with an electric mixer on medium speed for 2 to 3 minutes or until thick and lemon-color. Gradually stir about half of the remaining hot mixture into egg yolk mixture. Return egg yolk mixture to saucepan. Cook and stir over medium heat just until mixture returns to boiling. Remove from heat. Stir in 2 ounces grated white baking chocolate with cocoa butter until melted. Cover surface with plastic wrap; cool for 15 minutes. Stir before serving. Makes about ¾ cup.

Nut Pies and Tarts

5

Classic Pecan Pie ⏱

PREP 25 minutes BAKE 45 minutes COOL 1 hour OVEN at 350°F MAKES 8 servings

1   recipe Pastry for a Single-
     Crust Pie (see recipe, page 5)

3   eggs, slightly beaten

1   cup corn syrup

$\frac{2}{3}$ cup sugar

$\frac{1}{3}$ cup butter, melted

1   teaspoon vanilla

$1\frac{1}{4}$ cups pecan halves

1 Preheat oven to 350°F. Prepare Pastry for a Single-Crust Pie. On a lightly floured surface, use your hands to slightly flatten pastry. Roll pastry from center to edges into a circle about 12 inches in diameter. Wrap pastry circle around the rolling pin. Unroll into a 9-inch pie plate. Ease pastry into pie plate without stretching it. Trim pastry to $\frac{1}{2}$ inch beyond edge of pie plate. Fold under extra pastry even with the plate's edge. Crimp edge as desired. Do not prick pastry.

2 For filling, in a medium bowl lightly beat eggs with a fork. Add corn syrup, sugar, melted butter, and vanilla; stir until combined. Stir in pecans. Carefully pour the filling into crust.

3 Cover edge of pie loosely with foil. Bake for 25 minutes. Remove foil. Bake for 20 to 25 minutes more or until a knife inserted near the center comes out clean. Cool on a wire rack for at least 1 hour. Cover and chill within 2 hours.

NUTRITION FACTS PER SERVING:
532 cal., 34 g total fat (12 g sat. fat), 115 mg chol., 281 mg sodium, 54 g carb., 2 g dietary fiber, 24 g sugar, 6 g protein.

Make-Ahead Directions: Prepare as directed. Cover and chill for up to 2 days.

Chocolate-Pecan Pie

Add a dollop of whipped cream to this rich pie when serving.

PREP **45 minutes** BAKE **50 minutes** COOL **1 hour** OVEN at **450°F/350°F** MAKES **10 servings**

- **1** recipe Pastry for a Single-Crust Pie (see recipe, page 5)
- **4** ounces bittersweet chocolate, chopped
- **3** eggs
- **1** teaspoon vanilla
- **¾** cup packed brown sugar
- **¾** cup light-color corn syrup
- **½** cup unsalted butter
- **2** tablespoons all-purpose flour
- **¼** teaspoon salt
- **1½** cups pecan pieces

1 Preheat oven to 450°F. Prepare Pastry for a Single-Crust Pie. On a lightly floured surface, use your hands to slightly flatten pastry. Roll pastry from center to edges into a circle about 12 inches in diameter. Wrap pastry circle around the rolling pin. Unroll into a 9-inch pie plate. Ease pastry into pie plate without stretching it. Trim pastry to ½ inch beyond edge of pie plate. Fold under extra pastry even with the plate's edge. Crimp edge as desired. Generously prick bottom and sides of pastry with a fork. Line pastry with a double thickness of foil. Bake for 8 minutes. Remove foil. Bake for 6 to 8 minutes more or until golden. Cool on a wire rack. Reduce oven temperature to 350°F.

2 For filling, sprinkle chocolate on bottom of crust; set aside. In a large bowl lightly beat eggs and vanilla with a fork; set aside. In a medium saucepan combine brown sugar, corn syrup, butter, flour, salt and pecans. Cook and stir until mixture comes to boiling; boil for 15 seconds. Remove from heat. Quickly beat about 1 cup of the hot pecan mixture into eggs. Add egg mixture to remaining pecan mixture. Pour over chocolate in crust.

3 Cover edge of pie loosely with foil. Bake in the 350°F oven for 35 minutes. Remove foil. Bake about 15 minutes more or until edges are puffed and center appears set when gently shaken.

4 Cool on a wire rack for at least 1 hour. Cover and chill within 2 hours.

NUTRITION FACTS PER SERVING:
536 cal., 38 g total fat (17 g sat. fat), 117 mg chol., 134 mg sodium, 48 g carb., 3 g dietary fiber, 25 g sugar, 6 g protein.

125

Chocolate-Pecan Pie with Coffee Liqueur

PREP 40 minutes   BAKE 35 minutes   COOL 1 hour   OVEN at 375°F   MAKES 8 servings

- 1 recipe Pastry for a Single-Crust Pie (see recipe, page 5)
- ¾ cup semisweet chocolate pieces
- 3 eggs
- ¾ cup light-color corn syrup
- ½ cup packed brown sugar
- ¼ cup butter, melted
- ¼ cup coffee liqueur
- 1 tablespoon all-purpose flour
- 1 teaspoon vanilla
- 1 cup chopped pecans, toasted*
- ⅓ cup semisweet chocolate pieces, melted (optional)
- 1 recipe Coffee Whipped Cream (optional)

1 Preheat oven to 375°F. Prepare Pastry for a Single-Crust Pie. On a lightly floured surface, use your hands to slightly flatten pastry. Roll pastry from center to edges into a circle about 12 inches in diameter. Wrap pastry circle around the rolling pin. Unroll into a 9-inch pie plate. Ease pastry into pie plate without stretching it. Trim pastry to ½ inch beyond edge of pie plate. Fold under extra pastry even with the plate's edge. Crimp edge as desired. Do not prick pastry. Sprinkle the ¾ cup chocolate pieces over bottom of crust.

2 For filling, in a bowl lightly beat eggs with a fork. Add corn syrup, brown sugar, melted butter, liqueur, flour, and vanilla; stir until combined. Stir in pecans. Slowly pour filling over chocolate pieces in crust, spreading evenly.

3 Cover edge of pie loosely with foil. Bake for 25 minutes. Remove foil. Bake about 10 minutes more or until edge is puffed and a knife inserted near the center comes out clean. Cool on a wire rack for at least 1 hour. If desired, drizzle pie with the ⅓ cup melted chocolate. Cover and chill within 2 hours.

4 If desired, serve with Coffee Whipped Cream.

NUTRITION FACTS PER SERVING:
573 cal., 34 g total fat (13 g sat. fat), 110 mg chol., 271 mg sodium, 61 g carb., 3 g dietary fiber, 32 g sugar, 7 g protein.

Coffee Whipped Cream

Chill a large bowl and beaters of an electric mixer. In a chilled bowl combine ⅔ cup whipping cream and 1 tablespoon coffee liqueur. Beat with electric mixer on medium speed until soft peaks form (tips curl).

Make-Ahead Directions: Cover and chill for up to 2 days.

*tip
To toast nuts, preheat oven to 350°F. Spread nuts in a shallow baking pan. Bake for 5 to 10 minutes or until light brown, watching carefully and stirring once or twice.

⏱ Butterscotch-Pecan Tart

PREP 30 minutes BAKE 15 minutes COOL 1 hour OVEN at 450°/350°F MAKES 12 servings

1 **recipe Rich Tart Pastry (see recipe, page 6)**

3 **cups pecan halves**

1 **recipe Creamy Butterscotch Sauce**

⅔ **cup semisweet chocolate pieces**

⅓ **cup butterscotch-flavor pieces**
   Whipped cream (optional)
   Chocolate curls (optional)

1 Preheat oven to 450°F. Prepare and chill Rich Tart Pastry as directed. On a lightly floured surface, use your hands to slightly flatten pastry. Roll pastry from center to edges into a circle about 11 inches in diameter. Wrap pastry circle around the rolling pin; unroll into a 9-inch tart pan that has a removable bottom. Ease pastry into pan without stretching it. Press pastry into fluted sides of tart pan; trim edge. Prick pastry with a fork. Line pastry with a double thickness of foil. Bake for 8 minutes. Remove foil. Bake for 6 to 8 minutes more or until pastry is golden. Cool on a wire rack. Reduce oven temperature to 350°F.

2 For filling, toast pecans in the oven.* In a medium heatproof bowl combine warm pecans, 1¼ cups warm Creamy Butterscotch Sauce, the chocolate pieces, and butterscotch-flavor pieces, stirring until the pieces are melted.

3 Place the partially baked tart shell on a baking sheet. Carefully pour filling into tart shell. Bake in the 350°F oven about 15 minutes or until filling edges are bubbly. Cool on a wire rack for at least 1 hour. Remove side from tart pan. Serve with the remaining Butterscotch Sauce and, if desired, whipped cream and/or chocolate curls.

NUTRITION FACTS PER SERVING:
536 cal., 39 g total fat (14 g sat. fat), 76 mg chol., 127 mg sodium, 48 g carb., 4 g dietary fiber, 29 g sugar, 5 g protein.

Creamy Butterscotch Sauce

In a medium heavy saucepan melt ½ cup butter over low heat, stirring often. Increase heat to medium. Stir in ¾ cup light-color corn syrup, ⅔ cup granulated sugar, ⅔ cup packed dark brown sugar, 2 tablespoons water, and ¼ teaspoon salt. Bring to boiling, stirring constantly; reduce heat. Simmer, uncovered, for 5 minutes, stirring often. Remove from the heat. Carefully stir in ¾ cup whipping cream and 2 teaspoons vanilla. Serve warm. Cover and chill any remaining sauce for up to 2 weeks. Makes about 2⅔ cups.

*tip

To toast nuts, preheat oven to 350°F. Spread nuts in a shallow baking pan. Bake for 5 to 10 minutes or until light brown, watching carefully and stirring once or twice.

Banana-Pecan Caramel Tart

Offer a range of toppers for this pie—caramel topping, vanilla ice cream, or perhaps even offer the best of both of those worlds with caramel ice cream.

PREP 1 hour 10 minutes CHILL 1 hour FREEZE 20 minutes BAKE 30 minutes COOL 30 minutes OVEN at 400°F/350°F
MAKES 8 servings

1¼ cups all-purpose flour

1 tablespoon sugar

¼ teaspoon freshly grated nutmeg

⅛ teaspoon salt

½ cup cold butter

2 to 3 tablespoons ice water

4 small bananas, cut diagonally into ½-inch slices

1 cup pecan halves

2 eggs

½ cup sugar

3 tablespoons butter, melted

1 teaspoon vanilla

Caramel-flavor ice cream topping (optional)

Vanilla ice cream (optional)

1 In a large bowl stir together flour, 1 tablespoon sugar, nutmeg, and salt. Using a pastry blender, cut in ½ cup cold butter until mixture resembles coarse crumbs. Stir in the ice water, 1 tablespoon at a time, just until dough starts to form. Gather pastry into a ball, kneading gently until it holds together. Cover pastry with plastic wrap; chill for at least 1 hour or until easy to handle.

2 On a lightly floured surface, use your hands to slightly flatten pastry. Roll pastry from center to edges into a circle about 12 inches in diameter. Wrap pastry circle around the rolling pin; unroll into a 10-inch tart pan that has a removable bottom. Ease pastry into pan without stretching it. Press pastry into fluted sides of tart pan; trim edge. Freeze for 20 minutes.

3 Preheat oven to 400°F. Prick pastry with a fork. Line pastry with a double thickness of foil. Bake about 15 minutes or until pastry is set. Remove foil. Bake about 10 minutes more or until pastry is light brown. Cool on a wire rack. Reduce oven temperature to 350°F.

4 Place sliced bananas in pastry-lined tart pan. Top with pecans. In a small bowl lightly beat eggs with a fork. Add ½ cup sugar, 3 tablespoons melted butter, and vanilla; stir until combined.

5 Place tart pan on a baking sheet. Carefully pour egg mixture over banana and pecans. Bake in the 350°F oven about 30 minutes or until filling is set and slightly puffed. Cool on a wire rack for 30 minutes. Serve warm. Cover and chill within 2 hours.

6 If desired, drizzle each serving with caramel topping and serve with ice cream.

NUTRITION FACTS PER SERVING:
419 cal., 27 g total fat (11 g sat. fat), 95 mg chol., 167 mg sodium, 41 g carb., 3 g dietary fiber, 20 g sugar, 5 g protein.

Candied Sweet Potato-Lemon Pie

PREP 45 minutes   BAKE 15 minutes   COOL 1 hour   OVEN at 450°F/425°F   MAKES 8 servings

½   recipe Pecan Pastry

1   small lemon

¼   cup butter

2   pounds sweet potatoes, peeled and sliced ¼-inch thick

½   cup sugar

½   cup pecan halves

⅛   teaspoon ground nutmeg

Whipped cream (optional)

1 Prepare Pecan Pastry. Finely shred peel from lemon. Set aside.

2 In a straight-sided 12-inch skillet melt butter. Add sweet potatoes; stir to coat with butter. Cook over medium heat for 1 minute.

3 Sprinkle sweet potatoes with sugar; lift and fold sweet potatoes to coat and dissolve sugar. Cook for 5 to 8 minutes more or until caramelized and syrupy, stirring occasionally (do not stir too often or the sweet potato slices won't brown and caramelize). Stir in pecan halves, nutmeg, and finely shredded lemon peel. Remove from heat; let cool.

4 Preheat oven to 450°F. On a lightly floured surface, use your hands to slightly flatten one of the pastry balls. Roll pastry from center to edges into a circle about 12 inches in diameter. Wrap pastry circle around the rolling pin. Unroll into a 9-inch pie plate. Ease pastry into pie plate without stretching it. Trim pastry to ½ inch beyond edge of pie plate. Fold under extra pastry even with the plate's edge. Crimp edge as desired. Line pastry with a double thickness of foil. Bake for 8 minutes. Remove foil. Bake for 5 to 6 minutes more or until light brown. Cool on a wire rack. Reduce oven temperature to 425°F.

5 Carefully layer cooled potatoes in baked pastry shell (reserve syrup left in skillet). Bake in the 425°F oven for 15 to 20 minutes or until crust is golden and sweet potatoes are tender. Cool on a wire rack for 15 minutes.

6 Drizzle reserved syrup over top of pie. Cool for at least 45 minutes more. Cover and chill within 2 hours. If desired, serve with whipped cream.

Pecan Pastry

In a large bowl combine 2 cups all-purpose flour, ¼ cup ground pecans, and 1 teaspoon salt. Using a pastry blender, cut in ¼ cup shortening and ¼ cup butter, cut up, until pieces are pea size. Sprinkle 1 tablespoon cold water over part of the flour mixture; gently toss with a fork. Push moistened pastry to the side of the bowl. Repeat moistening flour mixture, using 1 tablespoon cold water at a time, until all of the flour mixture is moistened (½ to ⅔ cup cold water total). Gather flour mixture into a ball, kneading gently until it holds together. Divide pastry in half; form halves into balls. (Chill or freeze one of the pastry balls for another use. Chill for up to 3 days or freeze for up to 1 month. Thaw before using. Let chilled or thawed pastry stand at room temperature for 30 minutes before rolling out.) Chill the remaining pastry ball for 30 minutes before using. Makes enough pastry for two single-crust pies.

NUTRITION FACTS PER SERVING:
340 cal., 18 g total fat (7 g sat. fat), 23 mg chol., 252 mg sodium, 42 g carb., 4 g dietary fiber, 16 g sugar, 4 g protein.

Sweet Potato-Eggnog Pie ⏱

Eggnog season is far too short, so why not make good use of it by baking it into this perfect-for-the-holidays pie.

PREP **30 minutes** COOK **35 minutes** BAKE **50 minutes** COOL **1 hour** OVEN at **400°F/350°F** MAKES **2 pies (10 servings each)**

- 3 **pounds sweet potatoes**
- 1 **15-ounce package (2 crusts) rolled refrigerated unbaked piecrusts**
- 2 **tablespoons granulated sugar**
- ½ **teaspoon ground cinnamon**
- 1½ **cups eggnog**
- 1 **cup granulated sugar**
- 1 **cup packed brown sugar**
- 2 **eggs**
- ¼ **cup butter, melted**
- 2 **tablespoons brandy**
- 1 **teaspoon ground cinnamon**
- 1 **teaspoon vanilla**
- **Whipped cream (optional)**

1 In a covered Dutch oven cook sweet potatoes in enough boiling, lightly salted water to cover for 35 to 40 minutes or until very tender; drain. Cool until easy to handle.

2 Meanwhile, preheat oven to 400°F. Let piecrusts stand at room temperature according to package directions. Unroll piecrusts. Unroll each piecrust into a 9-inch pie plate. Ease each piecrust into pie plate without stretching it. Trim pastry to ½ inch beyond edge of each pie plate. Fold under extra pastry even with each plate's edge. Crimp edges as desired. Prick each crust with a fork. In a small bowl combine 2 tablespoons granulated sugar and ½ teaspoon cinnamon; sprinkle into crusts. Bake for 5 minutes. Cool on wire racks. Reduce oven temperature to 350°F.

3 Peel sweet potatoes; place in an extra-large bowl. Beat with an electric mixer on low speed until mashed. Add eggnog, 1 cup granulated sugar, brown sugar, eggs, melted butter, brandy, 1 teaspoon cinnamon, and vanilla; beat until combined. Divide evenly between partially baked pastry shells.

4 Bake in the 350°F oven about 50 minutes or until a knife inserted near centers comes out clean. Cool on wire racks for at least 1 hour. Cover and chill within 2 hours. If desired, serve with whipped cream.

NUTRITION FACTS PER SERVING:
290 cal., 10 g total fat (5 g sat. fat), 43 mg chol., 136 mg sodium, 47 g carb., 2 g dietary fiber, 3 g protein.

Cream Pies
and More

7

Spiced Sugar Cream Pie ⏱

Use a microplane to easily grate your fresh nutmeg.

PREP **25 minutes** BAKE **50 minutes** CHILL **2 to 24 hours** OVEN at **350°F** MAKES **8 servings**

1	recipe Pecan Pastry
¾	cup packed brown sugar
⅓	cup all-purpose flour
¼	cup granulated sugar
½	teaspoon grated whole nutmeg or ¼ teaspoon ground nutmeg
½	teaspoon ground cinnamon
	Dash ground cloves (optional)
2½	cups whipping cream
1	vanilla bean, split lengthwise, or 1 teaspoon vanilla
1	recipe Sugar Sprinkle (optional)

1 Preheat oven to 350°F. Prepare Pecan Pastry. On a lightly floured surface, use your hands to slightly flatten pastry. Roll pastry from center to edges into a circle about 12 inches in diameter. Wrap pastry circle around the rolling pin. Unroll into a 9-inch pie plate. Ease pastry into pie plate without stretching it. Trim pastry to ½ inch beyond edge of pie plate. Fold under extra pastry even with the plate's edge. Crimp edge as desired. Do not prick pastry.

2 In a large bowl combine brown sugar, flour, granulated sugar, nutmeg, cinnamon, and, if desired, cloves. Gradually stir in cream. If using, scrape seeds from vanilla bean. Stir vanilla bean seeds or vanilla into cream mixture.

3 Place the pastry-lined pie plate on the oven rack. Carefully pour cream mixture into pastry. Cover edge of pie loosely with foil.

4 Bake for 25 minutes. Remove foil. Bake for 25 to 30 minutes more or until filling is light brown and bubbly across the surface (pie will not appear set but will firm up upon cooling).

5 Cool on a wire rack. Cover and chill for 2 to 24 hours before serving. If desired, dust pie with Sugar Sprinkle.

NUTRITION FACTS PER SERVING:
584 cal., 42 g total fat (23 g sat. fat), 118 mg chol., 221 mg sodium, 48 g carb., 1 g dietary fiber, 27 g sugar, 5 g protein.

Pecan Pastry

In a medium bowl stir together 1¼ cups all-purpose flour, ¼ cup ground pecans, and ½ teaspoon salt. Using a pastry blender, cut in ¼ cup shortening and ¼ butter, cut up, until pieces are pea size. Sprinkle 1 tablespoon ice water over part of the flour mixture; gently toss with a fork. Push moistened pastry to the side of the bowl. Repeat moistening flour mixture, using 1 tablespoon ice water at a time, until all of the flour mixture is moistened (¼ to ⅓ cup ice water total). Gather flour mixture into a ball, kneading gently until it holds together.

Sugar Sprinkle

In a small bowl combine 1 tablespoon powdered sugar, ⅛ teaspoon grated whole nutmeg or dash ground nutmeg, and dash ground cinnamon.

Strawberry-Banana Cream Pie

PREP 35 minutes · BAKE 14 minutes · CHILL 1 to 6 hours · OVEN at 450°F · MAKES 8 servings

1	recipe Toasted Almond Pastry
½	cup sugar
2	tablespoons cornstarch
1¾	cups milk
2	egg yolks, lightly beaten
1	tablespoon butter
½	teaspoon vanilla
2	medium bananas
2	teaspoons lemon juice
2	cups sliced fresh strawberries
½	cup whipping cream
1	tablespoon sugar
¼	teaspoon almond extract

1 Preheat oven to 450°F. Prepare Toasted Almond Pastry. On a lightly floured surface, use your hands to slightly flatten pastry. Roll pastry from center to edges into a circle about 12 inches in diameter. Wrap pastry circle around the rolling pin. Unroll into a 9-inch pie plate. Ease pastry into pie plate without stretching it. Trim pastry to ½ inch beyond edge of pie plate. Fold under extra pastry even with the plate's edge. Crimp edge as desired. Do not prick pastry. Line pastry with a double thickness of foil. Bake for 8 minutes. Remove foil. Bake for 6 to 8 minutes more or until golden. Cool on a wire rack.

2 Meanwhile, for filling, in a medium saucepan stir together ½ cup sugar and cornstarch. Gradually stir in milk. Cook and stir over medium-high heat until thickened and bubbly; reduce heat. Cook and stir for 2 minutes more. Remove from heat. Gradually stir about 1 cup of the hot mixture into egg yolks. Return egg yolk mixture to saucepan. Bring to a gentle boil, stirring constantly; reduce heat. Cook and stir for 2 minutes more. Remove from heat. Stir in butter and vanilla. Cover surface with plastic wrap.

3 Cut bananas into ¼-inch slices; toss with lemon juice. Pour half of the filling into pastry shell, spreading evenly. Arrange half of the bananas and half of the strawberries on filling. Top with the remaining filling, bananas, and strawberries. Cover and chill for 1 to 6 hours.

4 Before serving, in a chilled medium bowl beat cream, 1 tablespoon sugar, and almond extract with an electric mixer on medium to high speed until stiff peaks form (tips stand straight). Pipe or spoon whipped cream on top of pie.

Toasted Almond Pastry

In a medium bowl stir together 1¼ cups all-purpose flour, ¼ cup finely chopped toasted almonds, and ¼ teaspoon salt. Using a pastry blender, cut in ⅓ cup shortening until pieces are pea size. Sprinkle 1 tablespoon ice water over part of the flour mixture; gently toss with a fork. Push moistened pastry to the side of the bowl. Repeat moistening flour mixture, using 1 tablespoon ice water at a time, until all of the flour mixture is moistened (3 to 4 tablespoons ice water total). Gather flour mixture into a ball, kneading gently until it holds together.

NUTRITION FACTS PER SERVING:
368 cal., 20 g total fat (8 g sat. fat), 82 mg chol., 119 mg sodium, 42 g carb., 3 g dietary fiber, 6 g protein.

187

Blueberry-Raspberry Tart with Lemon Cream

Whole wheat pastry flour will result in a slightly lighter texture than regular whole wheat flour, though both will work well.

PREP **25 minutes** CHILL **24 hours** BAKE **14 minutes** OVEN at **375°F** MAKES **10 servings**

1	recipe Lemon Cream
2/3	cup quick-cooking rolled oats
1/3	cup whole wheat pastry flour or whole wheat flour
1/3	cup all-purpose flour
1/2	of an 8-ounce package reduced-fat cream cheese (Neufchâtel), softened
1/4	cup butter, softened
1/4	cup sugar
1/4	teaspoon baking soda
1/8	teaspoon salt
1	teaspoon finely shredded lemon peel
1½	cups fresh blueberries
1½	cups fresh raspberries

1 Prepare Lemon Cream at least 24 hours before preparing tart.

2 Preheat oven to 375°F. Lightly grease a 10-inch tart pan that has a removable bottom; set aside. For pastry, in a small bowl stir together oats, whole wheat pastry flour, and all-purpose flour; set aside. In a large bowl beat cream cheese and butter with an electric mixer on medium to high speed for 30 seconds. Add sugar, baking soda, and salt. Beat until combined, scraping sides of bowl occasionally. Beat in as much of the oat mixture as you can with the mixer. Using a wooden spoon, stir in any remaining oat mixture and the lemon peel. Gather oat mixture into a ball.

3 Press pastry onto the bottom and up the sides of the prepared tart pan. Prick bottom of pastry with a fork. Line pastry with a double thickness of foil. Bake for 8 minutes. Remove foil. Bake for 6 to 8 minutes more or until pastry is golden. Cool on a wire rack.

4 Using a thin spatula or knife, loosen sides of pastry from pan. Remove sides of tart pan. Spread Lemon Cream evenly over bottom of tart shell. Top with blueberries and raspberries. If desired, cover and chill for up to 1 hour before serving.

NUTRITION FACTS PER SERVING:
216 cal., 9 g total fat (5 g sat. fat), 30 mg chol., 182 mg sodium, 31 g carb., 4 g dietary fiber, 6 g protein.

Lemon Cream

Line a yogurt strainer, sieve, or small colander with three layers of 100-percent-cotton cheesecloth or a clean paper coffee filter; place over a large bowl. Spoon one 16-ounce carton plain low-fat or fat-free yogurt* into strainer. Cover with plastic wrap; chill for 24 hours. Discard liquid in bowl. In a small bowl stir together the yogurt and 1/3 cup lemon curd. If desired, cover and chill for up to 3 days. Makes about 1⅓ cups.

*tip

Be sure to use a brand of yogurt that contains no gums, gelatin, or fillers. These ingredients may prevent the whey from separating from the curd to make yogurt cheese.

Fresh Fruit and Cream Tarts

Try using ripe and flavorful seasonal fruit and make this tart throughout the year.

PREP 40 minutes   CHILL 4 hours   BAKE 14 minutes   OVEN at 450°F   MAKES 8 individual tarts

1   recipe Pastry Cream

1   recipe Rich Tart Pastry
    (see recipe, page 6)

2   cups fresh fruit, such as
    raspberries, blackberries,
    sliced strawberries, and/or
    peeled and sliced papaya
    or kiwifruit

1 Prepare Pastry Cream; chill as directed.

2 Preheat oven to 450°F. Prepare Rich Tart Pastry as directed through Step 1. Divide pastry into eight portions. On a lightly floured surface, use your hands to slightly flatten each portion. Roll pastry from center to edges into circles about 5 inches in diameter. Transfer each pastry circle to a 4-inch tart pan that has a removable bottom. Press pastry into fluted sides of tart pans; trim edges. Prick pastry with a fork. Line pastry with a double thickness of foil. Place tart pans on an extra-large baking sheet. Bake for 8 minutes. Remove foil. Bake for 6 to 8 minutes more or until pastry is golden. Remove from baking sheet and cool on wire racks.

3 To serve, divide the chilled Pastry Cream among tart shells. Arrange fresh fruit on top of tarts. If desired, cover and chill for up to 4 hours. Remove sides of tart pans.

NUTRITION FACTS PER TART OR 1 WEDGE WHOLE TART VARIATION:
383 cal., 22 g total fat (13 g sat. fat), 210 mg chol., 186 mg sodium, 41 g carb., 1 g dietary fiber, 21 g sugar, 6 g protein.

189

Pastry Cream

In a medium heavy saucepan stir together ½ cup sugar, 4 teaspoons cornstarch, and ¼ teaspoon salt. Gradually stir in 2 cups half-and-half or light cream. If desired, add 1 vanilla bean, split lengthwise. Cook and stir over medium heat until thickened and bubbly. Cook and stir for 1 minute more. Gradually stir about half of the hot mixture into 4 lightly beaten egg yolks. Return egg yolk mixture to saucepan. Bring to a gentle boil; reduce heat. Cook and stir for 2 minutes. Remove from heat. Strain mixture into a bowl. If not using vanilla bean, stir in 1 teaspoon vanilla. Place bowl in a larger bowl of ice water and let stand for 5 minutes, stirring occasionally. Cover surface with plastic wrap. Chill about 4 hours or until cold; do not stir. Makes 2 cups.

Lemon Velvet Cream Pie

This chilled pie is a nice way to cool down on a warm summer day.

PREP **40 minutes** BAKE **22 minutes** COOL **1 hour** CHILL **2 hours** OVEN at **450°F/375°F** MAKES **8 servings**

1 recipe Pastry for a Single-Crust Pie (see recipe, page 5)
1 teaspoon unflavored gelatin
2 tablespoons cold water
6 egg yolks, lightly beaten
1½ 14-ounce cans (2 cups) sweetened condensed milk
¼ cup whipping cream
¼ teaspoon salt
¾ cup lemon juice
Whipped cream (optional)
Thin lemon peel slivers (optional)

1 Preheat oven to 450°F. Prepare Pastry for a Single-Crust Pie. On a lightly floured surface, use your hands to slightly flatten pastry. Roll pastry from center to edges into a circle about 12 inches in diameter. Wrap pastry circle around the rolling pin. Unroll into a 9-inch pie plate. Ease pastry into pie plate without stretching it. Trim pastry to ½ inch beyond edge of pie plate. Fold under extra pastry even with the plate's edge. Crimp edge as desired. Generously prick bottom and sides of pastry with a fork. Line pastry with a double thickness of foil. Bake for 8 minutes. Remove foil. Bake for 6 to 8 minutes more or until golden. Remove from oven. Reduce oven temperature to 375°F.

2 In a small microwave-safe bowl stir gelatin into the water; let stand for 5 minutes. Microwave, uncovered, on 100-percent power (high) for 14 seconds. Set aside.

3 In a large bowl beat egg yolks and sweetened condensed milk with an electric mixer on high speed for 2 to 3 minutes or until combined. Beat in gelatin mixture, cream, and salt on low speed until combined. Add lemon juice; beat on low speed for 30 seconds. Place the pastry shell on the oven rack. Carefully pour lemon mixture into pastry shell (pie will be full).

4 Bake for 22 to 25 minutes or until the center appears set when gently shaken. Cool on a wire rack for 1 hour. Cover and chill for at least 2 hours. To serve, top with whipped cream and garnish with lemon peel slivers.

NUTRITION FACTS PER SERVING:
558 cal., 32 g total fat (19 g sat. fat), 250 mg chol., 233 mg sodium, 59 g carb., 1 g dietary fiber, 40 g sugar, 11 g protein.

⏱ Honey Crunch-Chocolate Pecan Pie

PREP 30 minutes BAKE 50 minutes COOL 1 hour OVEN at 350°F MAKES 8 servings

1 recipe Pastry for a Single-Crust Pie (see recipe, page 5)

4 eggs, lightly beaten

1 cup light-color corn syrup

¼ cup granulated sugar

¼ cup packed brown sugar

2 1-ounce envelopes premelted unsweetened chocolate product

2 tablespoons butter, melted

1 tablespoon bourbon

1 teaspoon vanilla

½ teaspoon salt

1 cup chopped pecans

½ cup semisweet chocolate pieces

1 recipe Honey-Pecan Topping
Melted chocolate (optional)

1 Preheat oven to 350°F. Prepare Pastry for a Single-Crust Pie. On a lightly floured surface, use your hands to slightly flatten pastry. Roll pastry from center to edges into a circle about 12 inches in diameter. Wrap pastry circle around the rolling pin. Unroll into a 9-inch pie plate. Ease pastry into pie plate without stretching it. Trim pastry to ½ inch beyond edge of pie plate. Fold under extra pastry even with the plate's edge. Crimp edge as desired. Do not prick pastry.

2 For filling, in a large bowl combine eggs, corn syrup, granulated sugar, brown sugar, unsweetened chocolate product, melted butter, bourbon, vanilla, and salt; mix well. Stir in pecans and chocolate pieces.

3 Carefully pour the filling into the pastry-lined pie plate. Cover edge of pie loosely with foil. Bake for 25 minutes. Remove foil. Bake for 15 minutes more; remove from oven. Carefully spoon Honey-Pecan Topping evenly over pie. Return to oven. Bake about 10 minutes more or until topping is bubbly. Cool on a wire rack for at least 1 hour. Cover and chill within 2 hours.* If desired, drizzle with melted chocolate.

NUTRITION FACTS PER SERVING:
668 cal., 43 g total fat (13 g sat. fat), 127 mg chol., 360 mg sodium, 72 g carb., 5 g dietary fiber, 42 g sugar, 8 g protein.

Honey-Pecan Topping

In a small saucepan combine ⅓ cup packed brown sugar, 3 tablespoons butter, and 3 tablespoons honey. Bring to boiling, stirring constantly; reduce heat. Simmer, uncovered, for 2 minutes, stirring occasionally. Remove from heat. Stir in 1 cup pecan halves.

*tip
You can store the pie in the refrigerator for up to 24 hours before serving.

White Chocolate and Coconut Cream Pie

PREP 35 minutes   BAKE 10 minutes   CHILL 2 to 4 hours + 30 minutes   OVEN at 350°F   MAKES 8 servings

1	cup coconut
½	cup crushed graham crackers
¼	cup butter, melted
2	cups milk
1	cup coconut
6	egg yolks
¾	cup granulated sugar
½	cup all-purpose flour
1	tablespoon butter
2	tablespoons crème de cacao
4	ounces white chocolate (with cocoa butter) or white baking bar, chopped
1	tablespoon butter
2	cups whipping cream
½	cup powdered sugar
1	tablespoon crème de cacao (optional)
	Toasted coconut or white chocolate curls

1 Preheat oven to 350°F. For crust, in a medium bowl stir together 1 cup coconut, the crushed graham crackers, and melted butter. Press onto bottom and sides of a 9-inch pie plate. Bake for 10 minutes. Cool on a wire rack.

2 For filling, in a heavy large saucepan heat milk and 1 cup coconut just until simmering, stirring occasionally. Meanwhile, in a large bowl combine egg yolks, granulated sugar, and flour. Beat with an electric mixer on medium-high speed until combined. Gradually stir 1 cup of the hot milk mixture into the egg yolk mixture. Stir egg yolk mixture into the remaining milk mixture in saucepan. Cook and stir until boiling. Cook and stir for 2 minutes more. Remove from heat. Stir in 1 tablespoon butter and 2 tablespoons crème de cacao. Cover surface with clear plastic wrap. Cool completely.

3 Meanwhile, in a small saucepan combine white chocolate and 1 tablespoon butter; heat and stir over low heat until melted and smooth. Spread onto bottom and sides of cooled crust. Cool until white chocolate is firm.

4 Pour filling into crust. Cover and chill for at least 2 hours or up to 4 hours.

5 In a chilled large bowl combine whipping cream, powdered sugar, and, if desired, 1 tablespoon crème de cacao. Beat with an electric mixer on medium to high speed just until stiff peaks form (tips stand straight). Swirl whipped cream over chilled filling. Cover and chill for 30 minutes more. Top with toasted coconut or white chocolate curls.

NUTRITION FACTS PER SERVING:
683 cal., 47 g total fat (29 g sat. fat), 274 mg chol., 194 mg sodium, 57 g carb., 1 g dietary fiber, 8 g protein.

Grapefruit Tart with Chocolate-Almond Crust

PREP 55 minutes CHILL 3 to 4 hours OVEN at 375°F MAKES 12 servings

- 6 **ounces whole blanched almonds**
- 3 **tablespoons sugar**
- ¼ **cup butter, melted**
- 3 **ounces semisweet chocolate, chopped**
- ½ **cup butter**
- ¾ **cup sugar**
- 2 **tablespoons cornstarch**
- 1 **teaspoon finely shredded grapefruit peel**
- ½ **cup grapefruit juice**
- ½ **cup orange juice**
- ½ **cup whipping cream**
- 4 **egg yolks, lightly beaten**
- 1 **recipe Sweetened Whipped Cream (see recipe, page 31) (optional)**
- **Grapefruit sections and/or orange sections (optional)**

1 Preheat oven to 375°F. For crust, place almonds in a blender or food processor. Cover and blend or process until ground. In a small bowl combine ground almonds and 3 tablespoons sugar; stir in the melted butter. Press mixture evenly into the bottom and up the sides of a 9- to 9½-inch tart pan that has a removable bottom. Bake about 12 minutes or until golden. Cool on a wire rack.

2 In a small saucepan heat and stir chocolate over low heat until melted. Pour melted chocolate over crust, spreading evenly. Set aside.

3 For filling, in a medium saucepan melt ½ cup butter over medium heat. In a small bowl combine ¾ cup sugar and cornstarch; stir into melted butter. Stir in grapefruit peel, grapefruit juice, orange juice, and whipping cream. Cook and stir until thickened and bubbly. Cook and stir for 2 minutes more. Remove from heat. Gradually stir about 1 cup of the hot mixture into the egg yolks. Return egg yolk mixture to saucepan. Bring to a gentle boil; reduce heat. Cook and stir for 2 minutes.

4 Place saucepan in a large bowl of ice water; stir frequently until filling is cool. Pour cooled filling into baked crust, spreading evenly. Cover surface with plastic wrap; chill for 3 to 4 hours or until set.

5 To serve, remove sides of tart pan. If desired, top each serving with Sweetened Whipped Cream and grapefruit and/or orange sections.

NUTRITION FACTS PER SERVING:
345 cal., 26 g total fat (12 g sat. fat), 114 mg chol., 93 mg sodium, 27 g carb., 2 g dietary fiber, 22 g sugar, 5 g protein.

Dried Fruit Tart with Almond Crust

It's hard to decide which part of this sophisticated sweet is the best—the nutty pastry or the creamy filling topped with almonds and dried fruit.

PREP **45 minutes** CHILL **1 hour** BAKE **15 minutes** COOL **1 hour** STAND **30 minutes**
OVEN at **450°F/350°F** MAKES **8 to 10 servings**

1   **recipe Toasted Almond Pastry**

1   **recipe Sugared Orange Peel (optional)**

1   **3-ounce package cream cheese, softened**

½   **cup ricotta cheese**

1   **egg**

1   **tablespoon sugar**

1   **teaspoon finely shredded orange peel**

½   **cup dried tart red cherries, dried cranberries, and/or golden raisins**

¼   **cup boiling water**

½   **cup red currant jam or jelly**

¼   **cup slivered almonds, toasted**

1 Prepare Toasted Almond Pastry. If desired, prepare Sugared Orange Peel; set aside.

2 Preheat oven to 450°F. On a lightly floured surface, use your hands to slightly flatten pastry. Roll pastry from center to edges into a circle about 11 inches in diameter. Wrap pastry circle around the rolling pin; unroll into an 9-inch tart pan that has a removable bottom. Ease pastry into pan without stretching it. Press pastry into fluted sides of tart pan; trim edge. Line pastry with a double thickness of foil. Bake for 5 minutes. Remove foil. Bake about 5 minutes more or until pastry edge is light brown. Cool on a wire rack. Reduce oven temperature to 350°F.

3 Meanwhile, in a medium bowl combine cream cheese, ricotta cheese, egg, and sugar; beat with an electric mixer on low to medium speed until combined. Stir in shredded orange peel. Spread into partially baked crust. Cover edge of tart loosely with foil.

4 Bake in the 350°F oven about 15 minutes or until filling edge is slightly puffed and center is set. Cool in pan on a wire rack for at least 1 hour. Cover and chill within 2 hours.

5 Place dried fruit in a small bowl. Add the boiling water. Cover and let stand for 30 minutes. Drain well. In a saucepan heat and stir red currant jam over low heat until melted. Stir in dried fruit mixture and almonds.

6 To serve, remove sides of tart pan. Spread fruit mixture over cooled tart. If desired, garnish with Sugared Orange Peel.

NUTRITION FACTS PER SERVING:
309 cal., 16 g total fat (7 g sat. fat), 62 mg chol., 182 mg sodium, 38 g carb., 2 g dietary fiber, 22 g sugar, 6 g protein.

Toasted Almond Pastry

Preheat oven to 350°F. Place ⅓ cup slivered almonds in a shallow baking pan. Bake for 8 to 10 minutes or until toasted, stirring occasionally. Let cool. Place almonds in a food processor or blender. Cover and process or blend until finely ground. In a medium bowl stir together the ground almonds, ¾ cup all-purpose flour, 1 tablespoon sugar, and ¼ teaspoon salt. Using a pastry blender, cut in ¼ cup cold butter, cut up, until the pieces are pea size. Sprinkle 1 tablespoon cold milk over part of the flour mixture; gently toss with a fork. Push moistened dough to the side of the bowl. Repeat moistening flour mixture, adding an additional 1 tablespoon cold milk at a time, until all the flour mixture is moistened (2 to 4 tablespoons cold milk total). Gather flour mixture into a ball, kneading gently until it holds together. Wrap in plastic wrap; chill about 1 hour or until easy to handle.

Sugared Orange Peel

Using a vegetable peeler, remove the peel from an orange in thin strips, making sure not to get white pith. In a medium saucepan bring 1 cup water and ¼ cup sugar to boiling. Add peel. Simmer for 15 minutes; drain. On waxed paper or foil, spread peel in a single layer; sprinkle peel with sanding sugar. Let dry before using.

Make-Ahead Directions: Prepare as directed through Step 4. Cover with plastic wrap. Chill for up to 3 days. Continue as directed in Steps 5 and 6.

245

Harvest Fruit Tart

Serve this spiced pie with a scoop of vanilla ice cream.

PREP **40 minutes** BAKE **45 minutes** OVEN **at 375°F** MAKES **12 servings**

1   **recipe Pastry for a Double-Crust Pie (see recipe, page 5)**

1²⁄₃   **cups apple juice or apple cider**

³⁄₄   **cup snipped dried apricots or dried peaches**

³⁄₄   **cup snipped dried pitted plums (prunes)**

½   **cup dried tart cherries or raisins**

⅓   **cup packed brown sugar**

¼   **cup all-purpose flour**

¼   **teaspoon ground nutmeg**

1   **cup chopped, peeled cooking apple or pear**

½   **cup broken walnuts**

Milk (optional)

Granulated sugar (optional)

1 Preheat oven to 375°F. Prepare Pastry for a Double-Crust Pie. On a lightly floured surface, use your hands to slightly flatten one pastry ball. Roll pastry from center to edges into a circle about 13 inches in diameter. Wrap pastry circle around the rolling pin; unroll into a 10- or 11-inch tart pan that has a removable bottom. Ease pastry into pie plate without stretching it. Press pastry into fluted sides of tart pan; trim edge.

2 For filling, in a medium saucepan combine apple juice, apricots, plums, and cherries. Bring to boiling; reduce heat. Simmer, covered, for 10 minutes. Remove from heat. Meanwhile, in a large bowl stir together brown sugar, flour, and nutmeg; add chopped apple and walnuts. Gradually stir dried fruit mixture into apple mixture.

3 Transfer filling to pastry-lined tart pan. Roll remaining ball into a circle about 12 inches in diameter; cut into ½-inch-wide strips. Weave strips over filling into a lattice pattern. Press strip ends into bottom pastry on rim. Fold bottom pastry over strip ends; seal and crimp edge. If desired, brush pastry strips with milk and sprinkle with granulated sugar.

4 Bake about 45 minutes or until fruit is bubbly and pastry is golden. Cool on a wire rack. To serve, remove sides of tart pan.

NUTRITION FACTS PER SERVING:
333 cal., 15 g total fat (3 g sat. fat), 0 mg chol., 152 mg sodium, 47 g carb., 3 g dietary fiber, 23 g sugar, 4 g protein.

Holiday Fruit Pie

Quickly stir together cranberries and golden raisins for a pie that's as colorful as it is delicious.

PREP 35 minutes   CHILL 30 minutes to 24 hours   BAKE 45 minutes   COOL 1 hour   OVEN at 375°F   MAKES 8 servings

1   recipe Butter Pastry
1   12-ounce package fresh or frozen cranberries
2   to 3 teaspoons finely shredded orange peel
1   cup orange juice
½   cup golden raisins
½   cup dried cranberries
1   cup sugar
¼   cup all-purpose flour
1   egg, lightly beaten
2   to 3 teaspoons sugar

1 Prepare Butter Pastry. Preheat oven to 375°F. Meanwhile, for filling, in a medium saucepan combine fresh or frozen cranberries, orange peel, orange juice, raisins, and dried cranberries; bring to boiling over medium heat. Cook, uncovered, for 3 minutes. In a small bowl combine 1 cup sugar and flour; add to saucepan. Cook and stir until thickened and bubbly; cook for 1 minute more. Remove from heat.

2 On a lightly floured surface, use your hands to slightly flatten one pastry ball. Roll pastry from center to edges into a circle about 12 inches in diameter. Wrap pastry circle around the rolling pin. Unroll pastry into a 9-inch pie plate. Ease pastry into pie plate without stretching it. Transfer filling to pastry-lined pie plate. Trim pastry to ½ inch beyond edge of pie plate.

3 Roll remaining ball into a circle about 13 inches in diameter; cut into ½-inch-wide strips. Weave strips over filling into a lattice pattern. Press strip ends into bottom pastry on rim. Fold bottom pastry over strip ends; seal and crimp edge. Brush with egg; sprinkle with 1 tablespoon sugar.

4 Cover edge of pie loosely with foil. Bake for 25 minutes. Remove foil. Bake about 20 minutes more or until top is nicely browned and filling is bubbly. Cool on a wire rack for at least 1 hour. Serve warm or cooled.

NUTRITION FACTS PER SERVING:
608 cal., 34 g total fat (20 g sat. fat), 162 mg chol., 229 mg sodium, 73 g carb., 3 g dietary fiber, 7 g protein.

Butter Pastry

In a large bowl stir together 2½ cups all-purpose flour, 2 tablespoons sugar, and 1 teaspoon salt. Using a pastry blender, cut in ⅓ cup cold shortening and 6 tablespoons cold unsalted butter, cut up, until pieces are pea size. Sprinkle 1 tablespoon ice water over part of the flour mixture; gently toss with a fork. Push moistened pastry to the side of the bowl. Repeat moistening flour mixture, using 1 tablespoon ice water at a time, until all of the flour mixture is moistened (8 to 9 tablespoons ice water total). Gather flour mixture into a ball, kneading gently until it holds together. Divide pastry in half; form halves into balls. Flatten each ball into a disk; wrap in plastic wrap. Chill for at least 30 minutes or up to 24 hours.

247

Marzipan Tart with Fruit Tumble

Once upon a time, cooks had to grind almonds by hand to make almond paste. These days, you can find it in the baking aisle. Now that's progress! Crown this showpiece with the best-looking fruit at the market.

PREP 45 minutes   BAKE 30 minutes   STAND 1 hour   OVEN at 350°F   MAKES 8 servings

1   recipe Rich Tart Pastry (see recipe, page 6)

½   cup all-purpose flour

½   teaspoon baking powder

⅛   teaspoon salt

¼   cup butter, softened

½   of an 8-ounce can almond paste (½ cup)

⅓   cup sugar

1   teaspoon vanilla

3   eggs

¼   cup orange juice

2   tablespoons honey

2   teaspoons orange liqueur (optional)

3   cups orange sections, sliced nectarines, quartered strawberries, and/or whole raspberries, blackberries, or blueberries

Whipped cream (optional)

1   recipe Candied Orange Peel (optional)

1 Preheat oven to 350°F. Prepare Rich Tart Pastry. On a lightly floured surface, use your hands to slightly flatten pastry. Roll pastry from center to edges into a circle about 12 inches in diameter. Wrap pastry circle around the rolling pin; unroll into a 10-inch tart pan that has a removable bottom. Ease pastry into pan without stretching it. Press pastry into fluted sides of tart pan; trim edge. Set aside.

2 For filling, in a small bowl stir together flour, baking powder, and salt; set aside. In a large bowl beat butter with an electric mixer on medium speed for 30 seconds. Add almond paste, sugar, and vanilla; beat about 2 minutes or until smooth. Add eggs, one at a time, beating well after each addition. Add flour mixture; beat just until combined. Spoon into pastry-lined tart pan; spread filling to edges.

3 Bake for 30 to 35 minutes or until filling is puffed and golden. Cool completely in pan on a wire rack.

4 In a medium bowl stir together orange juice, honey, and, if desired, orange liqueur. Stir in fruit. Let fruit mixture stand for up to 1 hour.

5 To serve, remove sides of tart pan. Spoon fruit mixture over tart. If desired, serve with whipped cream and top with Candied Orange Peel.

NUTRITION FACTS PER SERVING:
456 cal., 25 g total fat (12 g sat. fat), 178 mg chol., 205 mg sodium, 53 g carb., 3 g dietary fiber, 29 g sugar, 8 g protein.

Maple Oatmeal Pie

If you like pecan pie, you'll love this rich maple and coconut pie.
Top it with cinnamon-spiked whipped cream for an unexpected taste.

PREP **25 minutes** BAKE **35 minutes** COOL **1 hour** OVEN **at 375°F** MAKES **8 servings**

- 1 **recipe Pastry for a Single-Crust Pie (see recipe, page 5)**
- 2 **eggs, lightly beaten**
- ¾ **cup pure maple syrup or maple-flavor syrup**
- ½ **cup granulated sugar**
- ½ **cup packed brown sugar**
- ½ **cup milk**
- ½ **cup butter, melted**
- 1 **teaspoon vanilla**
- 1 **cup flaked coconut**
- ¾ **cup rolled oats**
- ½ **cup chopped walnuts**
- 1 **recipe Cinnamon Whipped Cream (optional)**

1 Preheat oven to 375°F. Prepare Pastry for a Single-Crust Pie. On a lightly floured surface, use your hands to slightly flatten pastry. Roll pastry from center to edges into a circle about 12 inches in diameter. Wrap pastry circle around the rolling pin. Unroll into a 9-inch pie plate. Ease pastry into pie plate without stretching it. Trim pastry to ½ inch beyond edge of pie plate. Fold under extra pastry even with the plate's edge. Crimp edge as desired. Do not prick pastry.

2 For filling, in a large bowl combine eggs, maple syrup, granulated sugar, brown sugar, milk, melted butter, and vanilla. Stir in coconut, rolled oats, and walnuts. Pour filling into pastry-lined pie plate.

3 Bake for 35 to 40 minutes or until a knife inserted near the center comes out clean. Cool on a wire rack for at least 1 hour. Cover and chill within 2 hours.* If desired, serve with Cinnamon Whipped Cream.

NUTRITION FACTS PER SERVING:
618 cal., 33 g total fat (16 g sat. fat), 100 mg chol., 326 mg sodium, 76 g carb., 3 g dietary fiber, 49 g sugar, 7 g protein.

Cinnamon Whipped Cream

In a chilled medium bowl combine 1 cup whipping cream, 2 tablespoons powdered sugar, 1 teaspoon vanilla, ½ teaspoon ground cinnamon, and dash ground nutmeg. Beat with chilled beaters of an electric mixer on medium speed until soft peaks form (tips curl).

*tip
You can store the pie in the refrigerator for up to 2 days before serving.

Snickerdoodle Pie

It's always a good day when you turn a favorite cookie into a pie.

PREP **40 minutes**   BAKE **45 minutes**   COOL **30 minutes**   OVEN **at 350°F**   MAKES **10 servings**

1   recipe Pastry for a Single-Crust Pie (see recipe, page 5)

1   tablespoon raw sugar, coarse sugar, or granulated sugar

¾   teaspoon ground cinnamon

2   teaspoons butter, melted

½   cup packed brown sugar

¼   cup butter

3   tablespoons water

2   tablespoons light-color corn syrup

1½   teaspoons vanilla

¼   cup butter, softened

½   cup granulated sugar

¼   cup powdered sugar

1   teaspoon baking powder

½   teaspoon salt

¼   teaspoon cream of tartar

1   egg

½   cup milk

1¼   cups all-purpose flour

1 Preheat oven to 350°F. Prepare Pastry for a Single-Crust Pie. On a lightly floured surface, use your hands to slightly flatten pastry. Roll pastry from center to edges into a circle about 12 inches in diameter. Wrap pastry circle around the rolling pin. Unroll into a 9-inch pie plate. Ease pastry into pie plate without stretching it. Trim pastry to ½ inch beyond edge of pie plate. Fold under extra pastry even with the plate's edge. Crimp edge as desired. Do not prick pastry. In a small bowl combine the raw sugar and ½ teaspoon of the cinnamon. Brush the 2 teaspoons melted butter over pastry in pie plate. Sprinkle 1 teaspoon of the cinnamon-sugar mixture. Set aside.

2 For cinnamon syrup, in a small saucepan combine brown sugar, ¼ cup butter, the water, corn syrup, and the remaining ¼ teaspoon cinnamon. Bring to boiling over medium heat, stirring to dissolve sugar. Boil gently for 2 minutes. Remove from heat. Stir in ½ teaspoon of the vanilla. Set aside.

3 For filling, in a large bowl beat ¼ cup softened butter with an electric mixer on medium speed for 30 seconds. Beat in granulated sugar, powdered sugar, baking powder, salt, and cream of tartar until well mixed. Beat in egg and the remaining 1 teaspoon vanilla. Gradually beat in milk until combined. Beat in flour. Spread filling evenly in pastry-lined pie plate. Slowly pour cinnamon syrup over filling in pie plate. Sprinkle with the remaining cinnamon-sugar mixture.

4 Cover edge of pie loosely with foil. Bake for 25 minutes. Remove foil. Bake about 20 minutes more or until top is puffed and golden and a toothpick inserted near center comes out clean. Cool on a wire rack for at least 30 minutes.

NUTRITION FACTS PER SERVING:
423 cal., 20 g total fat (11 g sat. fat), 61 mg chol., 380 mg sodium, 55 g carb., 1 g dietary fiber, 27 g sugar, 5 g protein.

Coconut-Orange Tart

*The technique is French, and the flavors are pure tropical. Mixing classic cuisine with Creole touches,
the food of the French West Indies still differs from that of other Caribbean islands.*

PREP 40 minutes BAKE 35 minutes COOL 1 hour 30 minutes STAND 30 minutes OVEN at 350°F MAKES 12 servings

- 1 recipe Almond Pastry
- 3 eggs, beaten
- 1 cup sugar
- ⅔ cup flaked coconut
- ½ cup all-purpose flour
- 1½ teaspoons finely shredded orange peel
- 1 teaspoon vanilla
- ¾ cup butter, melted
- 3 oranges
- 1 cup chopped fresh pineapple
- 1 cup chopped papaya
- 1 tablespoon dark rum or 1 teaspoon vanilla
  Whipped cream (optional)
  Flaked coconut, toasted (optional)

1 Preheat oven to 350°F. Prepare Almond Pastry. On a lightly floured surface, use your hands to slightly flatten pastry. Roll pastry from center to edges into a circle about 12 inches in diameter. Wrap pastry circle around the rolling pin; unroll into a 10-inch tart pan that has a removable bottom. Ease pastry into pan without stretching it. Press pastry into fluted sides of tart pan; trim edge. Set aside.

2 In a large bowl combine eggs, sugar, ⅔ cup flaked coconut, flour, orange peel, and vanilla. Slowly add melted butter to egg mixture, stirring until mixed. Pour into the pastry-lined tart pan.

3 Bake about 35 minutes or until top of tart is crisp. Cool on a wire rack for at least 1½ hours. Cover and chill within 2 hours.

4 Peel and section oranges over a medium bowl to catch the juices. Add orange sections, pineapple, papaya, and rum to orange juice in bowl. Gently toss to mix fruit. Let stand for 30 minutes.

5 To serve, remove sides of tart pan. Cut tart into wedges. Using a slotted spoon, spoon some of the fruit mixture on top of each wedge. If desired, top with whipped cream and toasted coconut. Store any leftovers in the refrigerator.

Almond Pastry

In a medium bowl stir together 1¼ cups all-purpose flour, ½ cup ground toasted almonds, and ¼ cup sugar. Using a pastry blender, cut in ½ cup cold butter, cut up, until the pieces are pea size. In a small bowl stir together 2 egg yolks, beaten, and 1 tablespoon cold water. Gradually stir egg yolk mixture into flour mixture. Gather the flour mixture into a ball, kneading gently until it holds together. If necessary, cover with plastic wrap and chill for 30 to 60 minutes or until easy to handle.

NUTRITION FACTS PER SERVING:
*435 cal., 27 g total fat (15 g sat. fat),
143 mg chol., 245 mg sodium, 41 g carb.,
2 g dietary fiber, 5 g protein.*

251

Orange-Hazelnut French Silk Pie

PREP 40 minutes   STAND 20 minutes   CHILL 5 to 12 hours   OVEN at 350°F   MAKES 8 to 10 servings

6   ounces hazelnuts (filberts)

3   tablespoons packed brown sugar

2   tablespoons all-purpose flour

¼   cup butter, melted

1   cup whipping cream

1   cup semisweet chocolate pieces

⅓   cup granulated sugar

⅓   cup butter

2   egg yolks, lightly beaten

¼   cup hazelnut liqueur

1   teaspoon finely shredded orange peel (optional)

1   recipe Hazelnut Whipped Cream

1   recipe Candied Orange Peel (optional)

1 Preheat oven to 350°F. For crust, place hazelnuts in a food processor. Cover and process until finely ground. Add brown sugar and flour. With food processor running, add the melted butter through feed tube, processing until mixture holds together. Press mixture onto the bottom and up the sides of a 9-inch pie plate. Bake about 12 minutes or until crust is golden. Cool completely on a wire rack.

2 In a heavy medium saucepan combine whipping cream, chocolate pieces, granulated sugar, and ⅓ cup butter. Cook and stir over low heat about 10 minutes or until chocolate is melted. Remove from heat. Gradually stir half of the hot mixture into egg yolks. Return egg yolk mixture to chocolate mixture in saucepan. Cook and stir over medium-low heat about 5 minutes or until mixture is slightly thickened and begins to bubble. Remove from heat. (Mixture may appear slightly curdled.) Stir in liqueur and, if desired, finely shredded orange peel. Place the saucepan in a bowl of ice water; let stand about 20 minutes or until mixture stiffens and becomes hard to stir, stirring occasionally.

3 In a medium bowl beat chocolate mixture with an electric mixer on medium to high speed for 2 to 3 minutes or until light and fluffy. Spoon chocolate mixture into crust, spreading evenly.

4 Cover and chill for at least 5 hours or up to 12 hours. Spread Hazelnut Whipped Cream over chocolate layer. If desired, top pie with Candied Orange Peel.

NUTRITION FACTS PER SERVING:
700 cal., 57 g total fat (28 g sat. fat), 170 mg chol., 125 mg sodium, 44 g carb., 3 g dietary fiber, 36 g sugar, 6 g protein.

Hazelnut Whipped Cream

In a chilled medium bowl combine 1 cup whipping cream, 2 tablespoons sugar, 2 tablespoons hazelnut liqueur, and ½ teaspoon vanilla. Beat with the chilled beaters of an electric mixer on medium to high speed until soft peaks form (tips curl). Makes about 2 cups.

Candied Orange Peel

Using a vegetable peeler, remove peel from 2 medium oranges. Scrape away any soft white part inside the peel. (If white pith is left on, the peel will be bitter.) Cut peel into strips. Wrap and refrigerate peeled fruit for another use. In a 2-quart saucepan combine 1⅓ cups sugar and ⅓ cup water. Cover and bring to boiling. Add orange peel strips. Return to boiling, stirring constantly to dissolve sugar. Reduce heat. Cook, uncovered, over medium-low heat. Mixture should boil at a moderate, steady rate over entire surface. Cook about 15 minutes or until peel is almost translucent, stirring occasionally. Using a slotted spoon, remove peel from syrup, allowing it to drain. Transfer peel to a wire rack set over waxed paper. Set cooked peel aside until cool enough to handle but still warm and slightly sticky. Roll peel in additional sugar to coat. Continue drying on the rack for 1 to 2 hours before using. Store, tightly covered, in a cool, dry place for up to 1 week. (Or freeze for up to 6 months.)

Rhubarb-Raspberry-Apple Pie

*A trio of fruit flavors makes a delicious combination in this winning pie.
Using pastry cutouts in lieu of a top crust gives the pie a festive appearance.*

PREP 50 minutes BAKE 25 minutes OVEN at 450°F/375°F MAKES 8 servings

- 1 recipe Pastry for a Double-Crust Pie (see recipe, page 5)
- 1¼ cups sugar
- 3 tablespoons cornstarch
- 2 tablespoons all-purpose flour
- 4 cups chopped fresh rhubarb or frozen cut-up rhubarb
- 2 cups fresh raspberries
- 1 medium cooking apple, peeled and shredded (about ¾ cup)
- 1 to 2 tablespoons milk
- 2 to 3 teaspoons sugar (optional)

1 Preheat oven to 450°F. Prepare Pastry for a Double-Crust Pie. On a lightly floured surface, use your hands to slightly flatten one pastry ball. Roll pastry from center to edges into a circle about 12 inches in diameter. Wrap pastry circle around the rolling pin. Unroll pastry into a 9-inch pie plate. Ease pastry into pie plate without stretching it. Trim pastry to ½ inch beyond edge of pie plate. Fold under extra pastry even with the plate's edge. Crimp edge as desired. Line pastry with a double thickness of foil. Bake for 8 minutes. Remove foil. Bake for 5 to 6 minutes more or until light brown. Cool on a wire rack. Roll remaining ball into a 12-inch-diameter circle. Using a 2- to 3-inch cookie cutter, cut pastry into desired shapes. Cover cutouts loosely; set aside. Reduce oven temperature to 375°F.

2 Meanwhile, for fruit filling, in a large saucepan stir together 1¼ cups sugar, cornstarch, and flour. Stir in rhubarb, raspberries, and apple. Cook over low heat until fruit begins to juice out, stirring frequently. Increase heat to medium. Cook and stir over medium heat until thickened and bubbly.

3 Transfer fruit filling to the partially baked pastry shell. Brush edge of pie with milk. Place pastry cutouts over fruit filling and around the edge of the pie. Brush pastry cutouts with milk and, if desired, sprinkle with additional sugar. Bake in the 375°F oven about 25 minutes or until pastry is golden. Cool on a wire rack.

NUTRITION FACTS PER SERVING:
479 cal., 19 g total fat (7 g sat. fat), 15 mg chol., 336 mg sodium, 73 g carb., 4 g dietary fiber, 35 g sugar, 5 g protein.

Strawberry Sweetheart Tart

Start with purchased puff pastry, add a creamy filling, and top with romantic red berries—what a sweet and simple way to steal someone's heart.

PREP **35 minutes** BAKE **12 minutes** CHILL **1 hour** OVEN **at 375°F** MAKES **6 servings**

- ½ **of a 17.3-ounce package frozen puff pastry, thawed (1 sheet)**
- 1 **egg, lightly beaten**
- 1 **tablespoon water**
- ⅓ **cup sliced almonds, coarsely chopped**
- 2 **tablespoons sugar**
- ½ **cup whipping cream**
- 2 **3-ounce packages cream cheese, softened**
- 3 **tablespoons sugar**
- 2 **tablespoons amaretto or orange juice**
- ½ **teaspoon vanilla**
- 2 **cups sliced fresh strawberries**
- ¼ **cup currant jelly, melted**

1 Preheat oven to 375°F. On a lightly floured surface, roll puff pastry sheet into a 12-inch square. Using a sharp knife, cut pastry square into an 11-inch heart shape. Transfer heart to a baking sheet. Cut pastry trimmings into ¾-inch-wide strips. In a small bowl combine egg and the water. Brush egg mixture around top edge of heart into a ¾-inch-wide border. Twist pastry strips and arrange around top edge of heart to make a border, brushing ends with egg mixture and overlapping strips slightly. Brush pastry with egg mixture. Using a fork, prick center of pastry several times. Sprinkle pastry with almonds and 2 tablespoons sugar.

2 Bake for 12 to 15 minutes or until pastry is browned, pricking bottom once with fork if necessary to make it puff evenly. Cool on baking sheet on a wire rack.

3 For filling, in a chilled bowl beat cream with chilled beaters of an electric mixer on medium speed until soft peaks form (tips curl); set aside. In a medium bowl beat cream cheese and 3 tablespoons sugar with an electric mixer on medium speed about 1 minute or until fluffy. Add amaretto and vanilla; beat until well mixed. Fold whipped cream into cream cheese mixture. Spoon filling into cooled pastry shell, spreading evenly.

4 Arrange sliced strawberries over filling, overlapping to cover filling completely. Brush with melted jelly. Cover and chill for 1 hour before serving (do not chill any longer or the tart will be soggy).

NUTRITION FACTS PER SERVING:
505 cal., 35 g total fat (11 g sat. fat), 94 mg chol., 259 mg sodium, 42 g carb., 2 g dietary fiber, 7 g protein.

Key Lime Tart

PREP **40 minutes** BAKE **15 minutes** COOL **1 hour** CHILL **2 to 3 hours** OVEN at **450°F/350°F** MAKES **8 servings**

1 **recipe Rich Tart Pastry (see recipe, page 6)**

4 **egg yolks**

1 **14-ounce can sweetened condensed milk**

1 **teaspoon finely shredded lime peel**

½ **cup lime juice (10 to 12 Key limes or 4 to 6 Persian limes) or bottled Key lime juice**

Few drops green food coloring (optional)

1 **recipe Sweetened Whipped Cream (see recipe, page 31) (optional)**

1 Preheat oven to 450°F. Prepare Rich Tart Pastry. On a lightly floured surface, use your hands to slightly flatten pastry. Roll pastry from center to edges into a circle about 12 inches in diameter. Wrap pastry circle around the rolling pin; unroll into a 10-inch tart pan that has a removable bottom. Ease pastry into pan without stretching it. Press pastry into fluted sides of tart pan; trim edge. Line pastry with a double thickness of foil. Bake for 8 minutes. Remove foil. Bake for 6 to 8 minutes more or until pastry is golden. Cool on a wire rack. Reduce oven temperature to 350°F.

2 For filling, in a medium bowl beat egg yolks with a wire whisk or fork. Gradually whisk or stir in sweetened condensed milk; add lime peel, lime juice, and, if desired, food coloring. Mix well (mixture will thicken slightly).

3 Spoon thickened filling into baked tart shell. Bake in the 350°F oven for 15 to 20 minutes or until set in center. Cool on a wire rack for 1 hour. Chill for 2 to 3 hours before serving; cover for longer storage.

4 To serve, remove sides of tart pan. If desired, serve with Sweetened Whipped Cream.

NUTRITION FACTS PER SERVING:
330 cal., 15 g total fat (6 g sat. fat), 119 mg chol., 160 mg sodium, 42 g carb., 1 g dietary fiber, 9 g sugar, 7 g protein.

Shaker-Style Meyer Lemon Pie

PREP 45 minutes CHILL 8 to 24 hours BAKE 1 hour COOL 1 hour OVEN at 350°F MAKES 8 servings

- 4   Meyer lemons or regular lemons
- 2¼   cups sugar
- 1   recipe Pastry for a Single-Crust Pie (see recipe, page 5)
- 2   tablespoons all-purpose flour
- ¼   teaspoon salt
- 5   eggs
- ⅓   cup milk
- ¼   cup butter, melted
- 1   recipe Candied Lemon Slices (optional)

Candied Lemon Slices

Cut 2 Meyer lemons or regular lemons into ¼-inch-thick slices. Remove seeds. Roll slices in enough sugar to coat well (about ½ cup sugar). Coat a very large skillet with nonstick cooking spray; heat over medium-high heat. Arrange lemon slices in a single layer in skillet. Cook for 6 to 8 minutes or until sugar dissolves and lemon slices appear glazed (do not let them brown), turning once. Transfer to a piece of foil; cool completely. Roll cooled lemon slices in additional sugar before using.

1 Finely shred enough of the peel from 2 of the lemons to measure 2 tablespoons. Juice 1 or 2 of the lemons to measure ¼ cup juice. Cover and chill lemon peel and juice until needed. Peel the remaining 2 lemons, cutting away any white pith; discard peels. Very thinly slice all of the lemons crosswise. Remove seeds. Pour ½ cup of the sugar into a medium bowl. Top with lemon slices; sprinkle with another ½ cup of the sugar to cover completely. If necessary, gently toss to coat. Cover and chill for at least 8 hours or up to 24 hours.

2 Preheat oven to 350°F. Prepare Pastry for a Single-Crust Pie. On a lightly floured surface, use your hands to slightly flatten pastry. Roll pastry from center to edges into a circle about 12 inches in diameter. Wrap pastry circle around the rolling pin. Unroll into a 9-inch pie plate. Ease pastry into pie plate without stretching it. Trim pastry to ½ inch beyond edge of pie plate. Fold under extra pastry even with the plate's edge. Crimp edge as desired. Do not prick pastry. Set aside.

3 For filling, in a large bowl combine the remaining 1¼ cups sugar, the flour, and salt. In a medium bowl whisk together eggs, milk, butter, the reserved 2 tablespoons lemon peel, and the reserved ¼ cup lemon juice. Stir egg mixture into flour mixture until combined. Gently fold in the chilled lemon slice-sugar mixture. Pour filling into pastry-lined pie plate. Cover edge of pie loosely with foil.

4 Bake for 20 minutes. Remove foil. Bake about 40 minutes more or until evenly puffed and lightly browned (filling will still be jiggly). Cool on a wire rack for at least 1 hour. Cover and chill within 2 hours. If desired, top pie with Candied Lemon Slices.

NUTRITION FACTS PER SERVING:
478 cal., 16 g total fat (9 g sat. fat), 164 mg chol., 350 mg sodium, 83 g carb., 3 g dietary fiber, 59 g sugar, 8 g protein.

Lemon Sponge Pie

The candied lemon slices add a tart sweetness that complements this light and airy pie.

PREP **25 minutes** BAKE **30 minutes** COOL **1 hour** CHILL **3 hours** OVEN **at 450°F /425°F/350°F** MAKES **8 servings**

1 **recipe Pastry for a Single-Crust Pie (see recipe, page 5)**

2 **eggs**

1/3 **cup butter, softened**

1 **cup sugar**

2 **teaspoons finely shredded lemon peel**

1/4 **cup lemon juice**

2 **tablespoons all-purpose flour**

1/8 **teaspoon salt**

1 **cup milk**

1 **recipe Candied Lemon Slices (optional)**

1 Preheat oven to 450°F. Prepare Pastry for a Single-Crust Pie. On a lightly floured surface, use your hands to slightly flatten pastry. Roll pastry from center to edges into a circle about 12 inches in diameter. Wrap pastry circle around the rolling pin. Unroll into a 9-inch pie plate. Ease pastry into pie plate without stretching it. Trim pastry to 1/2 inch beyond edge of pie plate. Fold under extra pastry even with the plate's edge. Crimp edge as desired. Generously prick bottom and sides of pastry with a fork. Line pastry with a double thickness of foil. Bake for 8 minutes. Remove foil. Bake for 5 to 6 minutes more or until light brown. Cool on a wire rack. Reduce oven temperature to 425°F.

2 Separate egg yolks from whites; place whites in a medium bowl and set aside. In a large bowl beat butter with an electric mixer on medium speed until fluffy. Add sugar, beating until combined. Beat in egg yolks, lemon peel, lemon juice, flour, and salt just until combined. Add milk; beat just until combined (mixture will be thin and will appear curdled).

3 Thoroughly wash beaters. In the medium bowl beat egg whites on medium speed until stiff peaks form (tips stand straight). Fold beaten egg whites into lemon mixture. Spoon mixture into pastry shell.

4 Tent top of pie loosely with foil, making sure the foil does not touch the filling. Bake for 10 minutes. Reduce oven temperature to 350°F. Bake for 20 to 25 minutes more or until filling is set in the center.

5 Cool on a wire rack for 1 hour. Cover and chill for 3 hours. If desired, top with Candied Lemon Slices before serving.

NUTRITION FACTS PER SERVING:
351 cal., 18 g total fat (8 g sat. fat), 75 mg chol., 194 mg sodium, 44 g carb., 1 g dietary fiber, 27 g sugar, 5 g protein.

Candied Lemon Slices

In a small saucepan combine 1/4 cup sugar and 1/4 cup water. Bring to boiling. Add 1 lemon, very thinly sliced. Simmer gently, uncovered, for 12 to 15 minutes or until liquid is syrupy. Transfer lemon slices to waxed paper. Discard the syrupy liquid.

Lemon-Vanilla Tart

A sizable shot of vanilla brings out the sweet, flowery side of lemons.

PREP **40 minutes** BAKE **20 minutes** OVEN at **450°F/350°F** MAKES **8 servings**

1 **recipe Oven-Candied Lemon Slices**

1 **recipe Rich Tart Pastry (see recipe, page 6)**

2 **lemons**

½ **cup sugar**

1 **tablespoon all-purpose flour**

2 **eggs**

¼ **cup butter, melted**

1 **tablespoon vanilla**

1 Prepare Oven-Candied Lemon Slices; set aside. Preheat oven to 450°F. Prepare Rich Tart Pastry. On a lightly floured surface, use your hands to slightly flatten pastry. Roll pastry from center to edges into a circle about 11 inches in diameter. Wrap pastry circle around the rolling pin; unroll into a 9-inch tart pan that has a removable bottom. Ease pastry into pan without stretching it. Press pastry into fluted sides of tart pan; trim edge. Line pastry with a double thickness of foil. Bake for 8 minutes. Remove foil. Bake for 6 to 8 minutes more or until pastry is golden. Cool on a wire rack. Reduce oven temperature to 350°F.

2 Meanwhile, finely shred 4 teaspoons peel from the lemons; set aside. Squeeze enough juice from the lemons to measure 6 tablespoons; set aside.

3 In a medium bowl combine sugar and flour. Add eggs. Beat with electric mixer on medium to high speed about 3 minutes or until light in color and slightly thickened. Stir in the 4 teaspoons finely shredded lemon peel, the 6 tablespoons lemon juice, the melted butter, and vanilla. Pour into baked tart shell. Place tart pan on a baking sheet.

4 Bake in the 350°F oven for 20 to 25 minutes or until filling is set and lightly browned. Cool on a wire rack.

5 To serve, remove sides of tart pan. Top tart with Oven-Candied Lemon Slices.

NUTRITION FACTS PER SERVING:
338 cal., 19 g total fat (12 g sat. fat), 125 mg chol., 143 mg sodium, 40 g carb., 3 g dietary fiber, 20 g sugar, 5 g protein.

Oven-Candied Lemon Slices

Preheat oven to 275°F. Line a 15×10×1-inch baking pan with parchment paper. Cut 2 small lemons crosswise into ⅛- to ¼-inch-thick slices. Arrange lemon slices in a single layer on the prepared baking pan. Sprinkle lemon slices with ¼ cup sugar. Bake for 45 to 50 minutes or until lemons are almost dry and covered with a sugary glaze. While still warm, loosen slices from paper to prevent sticking. Cool completely.

Vanilla Tart with Berry-Orange Compote

If you'd like to try whole vanilla beans, this recipe is a great place to start. The filling and compote bring out the natural vanilla flavor, and the simple, classic technique of steeping the bean in hot milk is one you'll use often.

PREP **45 minutes** BAKE **30 minutes** CHILL **1 to 2 hours** OVEN **at 425°F/350°F** MAKES **8 servings**

1	recipe Hazelnut Pastry
¼	cup milk
1	vanilla bean, split lengthwise, or 1 teaspoon vanilla extract
3	eggs
1¼	cups sugar
⅓	cup butter
1	tablespoon cornstarch
1	recipe Berry-Orange Compote
1	recipe Vanilla Whipped Cream
	Chopped hazelnuts (filberts) or almonds, toasted (optional)

1 Preheat oven to 425°F. Prepare Hazelnut Pastry. On a lightly floured surface, use your hands to slightly flatten pastry. Roll pastry from center to edges into a circle about 12 inches in diameter. Wrap pastry circle around the rolling pin; unroll into a 9-inch tart pan that has a removable bottom. Ease pastry into pan without stretching it. (If pastry tears, overlap edges slightly and press smooth.) Press pastry into fluted sides of tart pan; trim edge. Line pastry with a double thickness of foil. Bake for 8 minutes. Remove foil. Bake for 4 to 5 minutes more or until set and dry. Set aside. Reduce oven temperature to 350°F.

2 For filling, if using the vanilla bean, in a small saucepan combine milk and vanilla bean. Heat just until boiling. Remove from heat; let stand for 10 minutes. Remove vanilla bean. If not using vanilla bean, stir together milk and vanilla. In a medium bowl beat eggs with a wire whisk just until mixed. Whisk in sugar. Set aside.

3 In a heavy medium saucepan heat butter over medium heat until butter turns the color of light brown sugar. Remove from heat; stir in cornstarch. Gradually add the vanilla-milk mixture and the browned butter mixture to egg mixture, stirring until mixed. Place tart pan on a baking sheet in oven. Pour filling into partially baked pastry shell.

4 Bake in the 350°F oven about 30 minutes or until filling is set in center. Cool in pan on a wire rack. Meanwhile, prepare Berry-Orange Compote.

5 To serve, remove sides of tart pan; cut tart into wedges. Using a slotted spoon, spoon Berry-Orange Compote over wedges; top with Vanilla Whipped Cream. If desired, sprinkle with chopped nuts.

NUTRITION FACTS PER SERVING: *550 cal., 29 g total fat (14 g sat. fat), 167 mg chol., 145 mg sodium, 69 g carb., 3 g dietary fiber, 52 g sugar, 7 g protein.*

Hazelnut Pastry

In a medium bowl stir together 1 cup all-purpose flour, $\frac{1}{2}$ cup ground toasted hazelnuts (filberts) or almonds, and 2 tablespoons sugar. Using a pastry blender, cut in $\frac{1}{3}$ cup cold butter, cut up, until pieces are pea size. In a small bowl combine 1 egg yolk, beaten; 1 tablespoon water; and 1 teaspoon vanilla. Gradually stir egg yolk mixture into flour mixture. Gather flour mixture into a ball, kneading gently until it holds together. If necessary, cover dough with plastic wrap and chill about 30 minutes or until easy to handle.

Berry-Orange Compote

Peel 3 oranges. Section oranges over a bowl to catch the juice. Add orange sections to juice in the bowl. Stir in $\frac{1}{4}$ cup honey and 1 tablespoon orange liqueur or orange juice. Add 2 cups sliced strawberries. Cover and chill for at least 1 hour or up to 2 hours. Stir before serving.

Vanilla Whipped Cream

In a chilled medium bowl combine $\frac{1}{2}$ cup whipping cream, 1 tablespoon powdered sugar, and $\frac{1}{4}$ teaspoon vanilla. Beat with the chilled beaters of an electric mixer on medium speed until soft peaks form (tips curl).

Vanilla Tart with Nutmeg Pastry and Vanilla Pears

Tahitian vanilla adds cherry flavor notes to this tart, making it a natural to pair with nutmeg. Other vanilla extracts would also work. Find Tahitian vanilla in specialty food stores or look for online sources.

PREP **40 minutes** CHILL **30 minutes + 2 to 8 hours** BAKE **20 minutes** COOL **1 hour** OVEN **at 350°F** MAKES **12 servings**

1 **recipe Nutmeg Pastry**
1 **recipe Vanilla Pears**
¼ **cup sugar**
8 **teaspoons cornstarch**
⅛ **teaspoon salt**
2 **cups half-and-half**
2 **teaspoons Tahitian vanilla extract or regular vanilla extract**

1 Position rack in lower third of oven. Preheat oven to 350°F. Prepare Nutmeg Pastry. Place pastry in a 9- to 9½-inch square or round tart pan that has a removable bottom. Using your fingers, evenly press pastry into a thin layer on bottom and sides of tart pan. (This takes patience, as there is just enough pastry to cover bottom and sides.) Chill for 30 minutes to firm the pastry.

2 Place pastry-lined tart pan on baking sheet. Bake for 20 to 25 minutes or until crust is a deep golden brown, checking after 15 minutes. If pastry has puffed from bottom of pan, prick a few times and gently press down with the back of a fork. Cool in pan on a wire rack.

3 Meanwhile, prepare Vanilla Pears. For vanilla filling, in heavy medium saucepan whisk together sugar, cornstarch, and salt. Add 3 tablespoons of the half-and-half; whisk to form a smooth paste. Whisk in the remaining half-and-half. Using a wooden spoon, stir constantly over medium heat, scraping bottom, sides, and corners of the saucepan until filling thickens and begins to bubble. Cook and stir for 1 minute more. Stir in vanilla extract. Immediately pour into baked pastry; smooth top. Cool on a wire rack for 1 hour. Cover and chill for at least 2 hours or up to 8 hours.

4 To remove, remove sides of tart pan. Serve with Vanilla Pears.

NUTRITION FACTS PER SERVING:
227 cal., 11 g total fat (7 g sat. fat), 33 mg chol., 91 mg sodium, 25 g carb., 1 g dietary fiber, 12 g sugar, 2 g protein.

Nutmeg Pastry

In a medium bowl combine 7 tablespoons unsalted butter, melted; ¼ cup sugar; ¾ teaspoon Tahitian vanilla extract or regular vanilla extract; ¼ teaspoon salt; and ⅛ teaspoon freshly grated nutmeg. Add 1 cup unbleached all-purpose flour; stir just until well mixed. If dough is too soft, let stand a few minutes to firm up.

Vanilla Pears

In a large saucepan combine 2 cups dry white wine or apple juice , ½ cup Poire William (pear liqueur) or pear nectar, 2 tablespoons sugar, and 1 vanilla bean, split. Bring to boiling; reduce heat. Simmer, uncovered, about 25 minutes or until reduced to 1 cup. Stir in 3 or 4 large firm ripe pears, sliced. Return to boiling; reduce heat. Simmer, covered, for 5 to 10 minutes more or until pears are crisp-tender. Remove from heat; cool. Chill until ready to serve.

Rustic Pies and Tarts

10

Maple-Cranberry Pies with Walnut Streusel Topping

PREP 45 minutes   BAKE 25 minutes   COOL 25 minutes   OVEN at 325°F   MAKES 12 pies

½ cup butter, softened

1 3-ounce package cream cheese, softened

1 cup all-purpose flour

¼ cup granulated sugar

1½ teaspoons cornstarch

1 cup fresh cranberries

¼ cup water

¼ cup pure maple syrup

¼ cup chopped walnuts, toasted*

¼ cup packed brown sugar

3 tablespoons all-purpose flour

2 tablespoons rolled oats

⅛ teaspoon salt

3 tablespoons butter

Vanilla ice cream (optional)

1 Preheat oven to 325°F. For pastry, in a medium bowl beat ½ cup butter and cream cheese with an electric mixer on medium speed until combined. Stir in 1 cup flour. Divide pastry into 12 equal portions. Press portions evenly into the bottoms and up the sides of 12 ungreased 2½-inch muffin cups. Bake for 15 minutes (pastry will shrink slightly as it bakes).

2 Meanwhile, in a small saucepan stir together granulated sugar and cornstarch. Add cranberries, the water, and maple syrup. Cook and stir over medium heat until thickened and bubbly, mashing berries slightly as they cook. Spoon mixture evenly into hot pastry-lined muffin cups.

3 In a small bowl stir together walnuts, brown sugar, 3 tablespoons flour, the oats, and salt. Using a pastry blender, cut in 3 tablespoons butter until mixture resembles coarse crumbs. Sprinkle evenly over filling in muffin cups.

4 Bake for 25 to 30 minutes or until tops are golden and filling is bubbly. Cool for 5 minutes in muffin cups. Carefully remove pies from muffin cups; cool on wire rack for 20 minutes to serve warm or cool completely on wire rack before serving.

5 If desired, serve with ice cream.

NUTRITION FACTS PER PIE: *238 cal., 15 g total fat (8 g sat. fat), 36 mg chol., 125 mg sodium, 25 g carb., 1 g dietary fiber, 13 g sugar, 2 g protein.*

*tip

To toast nuts, preheat oven to 350°F. Spread nuts in a shallow baking pan. Bake for 5 to 10 minutes or until light brown, watching carefully and stirring once or twice.

Petite Pies and Tarts

Mascarpone Cream Tarts

PREP 1 hour BAKE 10 minutes OVEN at 400°F MAKES 32 tarts

2 17.3-ounce packages (4 sheets total) frozen puff pastry, thawed

1 8-ounce carton (1 cup) mascarpone cheese, softened

1 recipe Pastry Cream

Sliced small carambola (star fruit) and/or sliced kiwifruit, cut into wedges (optional)

1 Preheat oven to 400°F. For tart shells, on a lightly floured surface, unfold one pastry sheet; roll lightly to minimize ridges. Using a 2-inch round cutter, cut 16 rounds. Repeat with remaining pastry sheets. Place half of the rounds on ungreased baking sheets; prick each a few times with a fork. Using a 1¼-inch round cutter, cut holes from centers from the remaining rounds; discard center cutouts.

2 Brush edges of rounds on baking sheets with water; top with remaining rounds. Press gently to seal layers together to form shells. Bake for 10 to 12 minutes or until puffed and golden. Transfer to wire racks; cool completely.

3 In a medium bowl beat cheese and chilled Pastry Cream with an electric mixer on low speed until smooth. Using your fingers, make an indentation in the center of each shell. (This allows more room for filling.) Carefully spoon cheese mixture into shells. If desired, arrange fruit on top of filled tarts. Cover and chill within 2 hours.

NUTRITION FACTS PER TART:
223 cal., 15 g total fat (5 g sat. fat), 29 mg chol., 84 mg sodium, 18 g carb., 0 g dietary fiber, 4 g protein.

Pastry Cream

In a medium saucepan stir together ⅓ cup sugar and ¼ cup all-purpose flour; gradually stir in 1 cup milk. Lightly beat 3 egg yolks with a fork; beat into flour mixture until smooth. Cook and stir over medium heat until thickened and bubbly. Remove from heat. Stir in 2 tablespoons clear crème de cacao, orange liqueur, raspberry liqueur, or 1 teaspoon vanilla. Pour into a medium bowl; cover surface with plastic wrap. Chill for 2 to 4 hours.

Make-Ahead Directions: Prepare as directed. Cover and chill for up to 1 hour before serving.

S'mores Ice Cream Pie

In a chilled large bowl use a wooden spoon to stir 2 pints (4 cups) chocolate ice cream until softened. Stir in 1 cup tiny marshmallows. Spread mixture evenly in a purchased graham cracker crumb pie shell or chocolate-flavor crumb pie shell.* Cover with plastic wrap and freeze for at least 4 hours or until firm. To serve, let pie stand at room temperature for 10 to 15 minutes before cutting into wedges. Meanwhile in a small saucepan cook and stir hot fudge ice cream topping over medium heat until warm. Sprinkle pie with additional tiny marshmallows. Drizzle with warm hot fudge ice cream topping. If desired, top each serving with Sweetened Whipped Cream (see recipe, page 31) and chopped honey-roasted peanuts.

NUTRITION FACTS PER SERVING: *376 cal., 16 g total fat (9 g sat. fat), 22 mg chol., 219 mg sodium, 54 g carb., 1 g dietary fiber, 5 g protein.*

Caramel-Butter Pecan Ice Cream Pie

In a chilled large bowl use a wooden spoon to stir 2 pints (4 cups) butter pecan ice cream until softened. Spread ice cream evenly in a purchased graham cracker crumb pie shell.* Cover with plastic wrap and freeze for at least 4 hours or until firm. To serve, let pie stand at room temperature for 10 to 15 minutes before cutting into wedges. Drizzle each serving with caramel ice cream topping. If desired, top each serving with Sweetened Whipped Cream (see recipe, page 31) and chopped toasted pecans.

NUTRITION FACTS PER SERVING: *340 cal., 16 g total fat (6 g sat. fat), 20 mg chol., 304 mg sodium, 48 g carb., 0 g dietary fiber, 3 g protein.*

Black Raspberry Cream Pie ⏱

Since the black raspberry jam is such a big component of this pie, be sure to go with a high quality jar (and taste it first to make sure you like it).

PREP **10 minutes**   FREEZE **4 hours**   STAND **5 minutes**   MAKES **8 servings**

1   **cup whipping cream**

1   **8-ounce package cream cheese, softened**

1   **10-ounce jar seedless black raspberry spreadable fruit**

1   **recipe Graham Cracker Crust (page 7)**

Fresh black raspberries (optional)

Lemon peel twist (optional)

Fresh mint (optional)

1 Chill a medium bowl and the beaters of an electric mixer. In chilled medium bowl beat whipping cream with electric mixer on medium to high speed until stiff peaks form (tips stand straight); set aside.

2 In a large bowl beat cream cheese with electric mixer on medium speed until smooth. Add spreadable fruit; beat until combined. Fold in whipped cream. Spoon cream mixture into Graham Cracker Crust.

3 Cover and freeze pie for at least 4 hours or until firm.

4 To serve, if desired, garnish with fresh black raspberries, lemon peel twist, and/or fresh mint. Place pie on a warm, damp towel for a few minutes before cutting into wedges.

NUTRITION FACTS PER SERVING:
438 cal., 30 g total fat (18 g sat. fat), 93 mg chol., 282 mg sodium, 39 g carb., 0 g dietary fiber, 27 g sugar, 4 g protein.

⏱ Blueberry Ice Cream Pie

This pie is proof that you don't have to make homemade ice cream in order to serve a stellar frozen dessert.

PREP 30 minutes BAKE 8 minutes FREEZE 3 hours + 8 hours OVEN at 350°F MAKES 10 servings

1½   cups slivered almonds
2   tablespoons packed light brown sugar
¾   teaspoon kosher salt
3   tablespoons unsalted butter, melted
⅓   cup granulated sugar
1   tablespoon water
1   teaspoon finely shredded lemon peel
2   teaspoons lemon juice
1   teaspoon cornstarch
¼   teaspoon grated fresh nutmeg
5   cups fresh blueberries
2   pints (4 cups) vanilla ice cream
½   cup whipping cream
½   cup crème fraîche or sour cream
1   tablespoon granulated sugar

1 Preheat oven to 350°F. In a food processor combine almonds, brown sugar and ½ teaspoon of the salt. Cover and process until almonds are coarsely ground. Transfer mixture to a small bowl and stir in the melted butter. Press onto bottom and up the sides of a 9-inch pie plate. Bake for 8 to 12 minutes or until golden. Cool on wire rack.

2 Meanwhile, for blueberry sauce, in a medium saucepan combine ⅓ cup granulated sugar, the water, lemon peel, lemon juice, cornstarch, the remaining ¼ teaspoon salt, and the nutmeg; add 3 cups of the blueberries. Cook, stirring occasionally, until berries pop and mixture comes to boiling. Reduce heat; boil gently, uncovered, for 2 minutes. Transfer to a bowl; cover and chill.

3 In a chilled large bowl use a wooden spoon to stir half of the ice cream until softened. Spread evenly in the prepared crust. Cover with plastic wrap and freeze for at least 2 hours or until firm. Add ¾ cup of the blueberry sauce, spreading evenly; freeze for at least 1 hour or until set. Use a wooden spoon to stir the remaining ice cream until softened and add to pie, spreading evenly. Cover with plastic wrap and freeze for at least 8 hours or until very firm.

4 Chill a medium bowl and the beaters of an electric mixer. Just before serving, in a chilled bowl beat cream, crème fraîche, and 1 tablespoon sugar with an electric mixer until soft peaks form (tips curl). Spread evenly over pie and top with the remaining 2 cups blueberries.

5 To serve, in a small saucepan cook and stir the remaining blueberry sauce over medium heat until warm. Cut pie into wedges and serve warm blueberry sauce with pie.

NUTRITION FACTS PER SERVING:
363 cal., 22 g total fat (10 g sat. fat), 53 mg chol., 200 mg sodium, 39 g carb., 4 g dietary fiber, 31 g sugar, 6 g protein.

Devil's Food Ice Cream Pie ⏱

Add the chocolate topping after freezing the pie—otherwise, the chocolate flavor will not be as strong.

PREP 20 minutes FREEZE 8 hours STAND 10 minutes MAKES 12 servings

1 6.75-ounce package fat-free devil's food cookie cakes (12 cookies)

¼ cup peanut butter

¼ cup hot water

2 pints (4 cups) vanilla, chocolate, or desired flavor ice cream

1 cup sliced banana (about 1 large)

3 tablespoons hot fudge ice cream topping

1 Coarsely chop cookies. Place cookie pieces in the bottom of an 8-inch springform pan. In a small bowl whisk together peanut butter and the hot water until smooth. Drizzle evenly over cookies.

2 In a chilled large bowl use a wooden spoon to stir ice cream until softened. Top cookie layer with banana slices and carefully spoon ice cream evenly over all, spreading until smooth on top. Cover with plastic wrap; freeze about 8 hours or until firm.

3 To serve, let stand at room temperature for 10 minutes. Remove sides of the pan; cut pie into wedges. Drizzle fudge topping over each serving.

NUTRITION FACTS PER SERVING:
208 cal., 9 g total fat (4 g sat. fat), 21 mg chol., 99 mg sodium, 30 g carb., 1 g dietary fiber, 21 g sugar, 4 g protein.

Chocolate Crisp-Crust Ice Cream Pie ⏱

The crisp rice cereal makes for a crunchy contrast to the smooth ice cream.

PREP 30 minutes FREEZE 15 minutes + 2 hours STAND 10 minutes MAKES 8 servings

½ cup semisweet chocolate pieces

½ cup milk chocolate pieces

2 cups crisp rice cereal

¾ cup finely chopped unsalted roasted peanuts

¾ cup chocolate toffee bits

¾ cup shredded coconut

2 pints (4 cups) vanilla ice cream

1 In a large microwave-safe bowl combine semisweet chocolate pieces and milk chocolate pieces. Microwave on 100-percent power (high) for 30 seconds; stir. Repeat heating and stirring two to three more times or until chocolate is melted and smooth. Add cereal, ¼ cup of the peanuts, ¼ cup of the toffee bits, and ¼ cup of the coconut. Stir to coat evenly.

2 Butter a 9-inch pie plate. Using your hands or a wooden spoon, press chocolate mixture into the bottom and up the sides of the pie plate. Freeze for 15 minutes to firm.

3 In a chilled large bowl use a wooden spoon to stir ice cream until softened. Stir in the remaining ½ cup peanuts, the remaining ½ cup toffee bits, and the remaining ½ cup coconut. Spread ice cream mixture into piecrust. Cover with plastic wrap and freeze for at least 2 hours or until firm.

4 To serve, let stand at room temperature for 10 minutes.

NUTRITION FACTS PER SERVING:
559 cal., 33 g total fat (17 g sat. fat), 42 mg chol., 249 mg sodium, 59 g carb., 2 g dietary fiber, 47 g sugar, 8 g protein.

Coffee-Chocolate Cherry Ice Box Pie

Consider making two of these scrumptious icebox pies—they keep beautifully when tightly wrapped and frozen, which means they're ready to grab when an impromptu grill-out ends up in your yard.

PREP **35 minutes** FREEZE **30 minutes + 4 hours** STAND **10 minutes** MAKES **8 servings**

1 **pint (2 cups) coffee-flavor frozen yogurt or ice cream**

1 **purchased chocolate cookie crumb pie shell or chocolate-flavor crumb pie shell**

⅓ **cup light chocolate-flavor syrup or hot fudge sauce**

1 **pint vanilla frozen yogurt or ice cream**

1 **cup fresh sweet cherries, pitted and chopped, or ½ cup chopped frozen pitted sweet cherries**

¼ **cup chopped, toasted almonds**

1 **recipe Chocolate-Dipped Cherries; 1 cup fresh sweet cherries with stems, pitted; or 1 cup frozen pitted sweet cherries, thawed**

1 In a chilled large bowl use a wooden spoon to stir coffee frozen yogurt until softened. Spread evenly in pie shell. Drizzle with chocolate-flavor syrup. Cover and freeze for 30 minutes.

2 In a chilled large bowl use a wooden spoon to stir vanilla frozen yogurt until softened. Stir in chopped cherries and almonds until combined. Spread mixture evenly over frozen coffee layer in pie shell. Cover with plastic wrap and freeze for at least 4 hours or until firm.

3 To serve, top with Chocolate-Dipped Cherries. Let pie stand at room temperature for 10 to 20 minutes before cutting into wedges.

NUTRITION FACTS PER SERVING:
398 cal., 15 g total fat (7 g sat. fat), 38 mg chol., 202 mg sodium, 59 g carb., 2 g dietary fiber, 32 g sugar, 9 g protein.

Chocolate-Dipped Cherries

Pit 1 cup (about 16) fresh sweet cherries, leaving stems intact. Pat dry with paper towels; set aside. In a small saucepan melt 2 ounces chopped bittersweet chocolate and 2 ounces chopped chocolate-flavor candy coating. Holding cherries by stems, dip into chocolate mixture to coat. Let stand on waxed paper until set.

Make-Ahead Directions: Prepare as directed. Wrap pie tightly in freezer wrap. Freeze for up to 2 months.

Frozen Peanut Butter Pie ⏱

Starting with room temperature peanut butter will make measuring it out a lot easier.

PREP 15 minutes   FREEZE 3 hours   MAKES 12 servings

2¼   cups whipping cream

1¼   cups creamy or chunky peanut butter

1   cup powdered sugar

1   cup (about 15) chopped bite-size chocolate-covered peanut butter cups

1   purchased chocolate cookie crumb pie shell

6   chocolate-covered peanut butter cups, halved

1 In a small saucepan combine ¼ cup of the cream, the peanut butter, and ¼ cup of the powdered sugar. Cook and stir over medium heat until smooth. Cool to room temperature.

2 Meanwhile, in a chilled medium bowl combine the remaining 2 cups cream and the remaining ¾ cup powdered sugar. Beat with an electric mixer on medium speed until stiff peaks form (tips stand straight).

3 Fold peanut butter mixture into whipped cream mixture. Fold in the chopped peanut butter cups. Spoon mixture into pie shell. Top with the halved peanut butter cups. Cover with plastic wrap and freeze about 3 hours or until nearly firm.

NUTRITION FACTS PER SERVING:
464 cal., 36 g total fat (15 g sat. fat), 63 mg chol., 243 mg sodium, 30 g carb., 2 g dietary fiber, 9 g protein.

Frozen White Chocolate-Cranberry Pie ⏱

This pie makes for an unexpected holiday dessert, especially when paired with warm coffee.

PREP 20 minutes   COOL 30 minutes   FREEZE 15 minutes + 6 hours   STAND 15 minutes   MAKES 8 servings

2   ounces white chocolate baking squares or white baking bars, coarsely chopped

1   3-ounce package cream cheese, cut up

1   purchased shortbread crumb pie shell

2   pints (4 cups) vanilla ice cream

½   cup chopped dried cranberries

¼   cup chopped pecans, toasted
    Dried cranberries (optional)
    Chopped toasted pecans (optional)

1 In a small saucepan combine white chocolate and cream cheese; cook and stir over low heat until melted and smooth. Cool about 30 minutes or until room temperature. Spread white chocolate mixture in the bottom of the pie shell. Freeze for 15 minutes until firm.

2 In a chilled large bowl use a wooden spoon to stir ice cream until softened; fold in ½ cup cranberries and ¼ cup pecans. Spread evenly in pie shell. Cover with plastic wrap and freeze for at least 6 hours or until firm.

3 To serve, let stand at room temperature for 15 minutes. If desired, top with additional cranberries and pecans.

NUTRITION FACTS PER SERVING:
419 cal., 28 g total fat (13 g sat. fat), 67 mg chol., 195 mg sodium, 38 g carb., 1 g dietary fiber, 17 g sugar, 5 g protein.

⏱ Peanut Butter and Ice Cream Pie

This frosty peanut butter pie gets a double dose of chocolate—in the crust and in the warm topping.

PREP 25 minutes   FREEZE 10 minutes + 4 hours   STAND 5 minutes   MAKES 8 servings

1¼   cups finely crushed chocolate sandwich cookies with white filling*

¼   cup butter, melted*

2   pints (4 cups) vanilla ice cream

½   of an 8-ounce container frozen whipped dessert topping, thawed

½   cup chunky peanut butter

½   cup hot fudge ice cream topping

¼   cup chopped peanuts (optional)

1 For crust, in a medium bowl combine crushed cookies and melted butter. Press mixture evenly onto the bottom and up the sides of a 9-inch pie plate. Cover and freeze about 10 minutes or until firm.

2 For filling, in a chilled large bowl use a wooden spoon to stir ice cream until softened. Fold in whipped topping. Fold in peanut butter just until combined. Spread filling evenly in prepared piecrust. Cover with plastic wrap and freeze for at least 4 hours or until firm.

3 To serve, place the pie on a warm, damp towel for 5 minutes before cutting into wedges. In a small saucepan cook and stir hot fudge topping over medium heat until warm. Drizzle each serving with warm topping and, if desired, sprinkle with peanuts.

NUTRITION FACTS PER SERVING:
603 cal., 38 g total fat (20 g sat. fat), 114 mg chol., 317 mg sodium, 58 g carb., 2 g dietary fiber, 42 g sugar, 9 g protein.

*tip
If desired, substitute 1¼ cups finely crushed chocolate graham crackers for the chocolate sandwich cookies and increase melted butter to ⅓ cup.

Ice Cream Pies

Soda Fountain Ice Cream Pie ⏱

Crushed sugar ice cream cones are the secret to the crunchy crust for this luscious ice cream pie.

PREP **20 minutes** FREEZE **1½ hours + 8 hours** STAND **15 minutes** MAKES **10 servings**

1½   **cups crushed rolled sugar ice cream cones (12 cones)**

¼   **cup sugar**

½   **cup butter, melted**

3   **cups fresh strawberries**

2   **pints (4 cups) vanilla ice cream**

⅓   **cup malted milk powder**

½   **cup finely chopped fresh strawberries**

1   **recipe Sweetened Whipped Cream (see recipe, page 31) (optional)**

Malted milk balls, coarsely chopped (optional)

Fresh strawberries (optional)

Hot fudge ice cream topping (optional)

1 For crust, in a medium bowl combine crushed cones and sugar. Drizzle with melted butter; gently toss to coat. Press mixture evenly onto bottom of an 8- or 9-inch springform pan. Cover and freeze about 30 minutes or until firm.

2 Meanwhile, place 3 cups strawberries in a blender. Cover and blend until smooth.

3 In a chilled large bowl use a wooden spoon to stir ice cream until softened. Stir in ½ cup of the pureed strawberries and the malted milk powder. Spread half of the mixture evenly in crust. Cover and freeze for 30 minutes. (Cover and freeze remaining ice cream mixture.)

4 Spoon remaining pureed strawberries over ice cream layer. Cover and freeze for 30 minutes more. Use a wooden spoon to stir remaining ice cream mixture until softened. Spread evenly over strawberry layer. Top with ½ cup chopped strawberries. Cover with plastic wrap and freeze for at least 8 hours or until firm.

5 To serve, let pie stand at room temperature for 15 minutes before cuttting into wedges. If desired, top each serving with Sweetened Whipped Cream, malted milk balls, and additional strawberries. If desired, serve with hot fudge topping.

NUTRITION FACTS PER SERVING:
308 cal., 17 g total fat (10 g sat. fat), 52 mg chol., 178 mg sodium, 37 g carb., 2 g dietary fiber, 25 g sugar, 4 g protein.

Lower Calorie

13

Key Lime Pie ⏱

PREP 30 minutes BAKE 8 minutes CHILL 30 minutes + 4 hours OVEN at 350°F MAKES 8 servings

1½ **cups small pretzel twists (about 34)**

2 **tablespoons sliced almonds, toasted***

3 **tablespoons butter, melted**

1 **3-ounce package (4-serving-size) sugar-free lime-flavor gelatin or regular lime-flavor gelatin**

1 **cup boiling water**

2 **6-ounce cartons low-fat key lime pie-flavor yogurt**

½ **of an 8-ounce container frozen light whipped dessert topping, thawed**

1 **teaspoon finely shredded lime peel**

Finely shredded lime peel and/or raspberries (optional)

1 Preheat oven to 350°F. For crust, in a food processor combine pretzels and almonds. Cover and process until finely crushed. Add melted butter; cover and process until combined. Press pretzel mixture onto bottom and up the sides of a 9-inch pie plate. Bake for 8 to 10 minutes or until light brown. Cool on a wire rack.

2 In a medium bowl combine gelatin and the boiling water; stir about 2 minutes or until gelatin is dissolved. Cover and chill about 30 minutes or until mixture is partially set (the consistency of unbeaten egg whites). Fold in yogurt, whipped topping, and 1 teaspoon lime peel. Spoon into cooled crust.

3 Chill for at least 4 hours. If desired, garnish with additional lime peel and/or raspberries.

NUTRITION FACTS PER SERVING:
153 cal., 7 g total fat (5 g sat. fat), 13 mg chol., 180 mg sodium, 17 g carb., 0 g dietary fiber, 10 g sugar, 3 g protein.

*tip

To toast nuts, preheat oven to 350°F. Spread nuts in a shallow baking pan. Bake for 5 to 10 minutes or until light brown, watching carefully and stirring once or twice.

Pear-Cranberry Deep-Dish Pie

Cranberries give this full-of-fruit pie a rosy hue and a hint of tartness.

PREP 40 minutes   BAKE 55 minutes   COOL 30 minutes   OVEN at 375°F   MAKES 10 servings

1/3   cup granulated sugar

2   tablespoons all-purpose flour

1/4   teaspoon ground nutmeg

1/4   teaspoon ground ginger

6   cups sliced, cored pears
(2 to 2½ pounds total)

1   cup fresh or thawed frozen
cranberries

1   recipe Pastry

1   tablespoon fat-free milk

Demerara sugar or raw sugar
(optional)

1 Preheat oven to 375°F. Line a baking sheet with foil; set aside. In a very large bowl combine granulated sugar, flour, nutmeg, and ginger. Add pear slices and cranberries; toss to coat. Transfer to a 2-quart round baking dish or casserole.

2 Prepare Pastry. On a lightly floured surface, use your hands to slightly flatten pastry. Roll pastry from center to edges into a circle that is about 1 inch wider than the top of the baking dish or casserole. Using cookie cutters, cut a few small shapes from center of the pastry. Set shapes aside. Wrap pastry circle around rolling pin. Unroll on top of fruit mixture. Trim pastry as needed to fit the baking dish or casserole. If desired, crimp edge. Brush top of pastry and pastry cutouts with milk. Place cutouts on pastry, leaving openings for air to vent.

3 Place baking dish or casserole on the prepared baking sheet. If desired, sprinkle with demerara sugar. Bake for 55 to 60 minutes or until pear mixture is bubbly. Cool pie on a wire rack for 30 minutes. Serve warm or cool completely on a wire rack.

NUTRITION FACTS PER SERVING:
169 cal., 4 g total fat (1 g sat. fat), 0 mg chol., 96 mg sodium, 34 g carb., 4 g dietary fiber, 16 g sugar, 2 g protein.

Pastry

In a medium bowl stir together ¾ cup cake flour, ¼ cup whole wheat flour, and ¼ teaspoon salt. Using a pastry blender, cut in ¼ cup cold butter, cut up, until pieces are pea size. Sprinkle 1 tablespoon ice water over part of the flour mixture; gently toss with a fork. Push moistened pastry to side of bowl. Repeat moistening flour mixture, using 1 tablespoon ice water at a time, until all of the flour mixture is moistened (3 to 4 tablespoons total). Gather flour mixture into a ball, kneading gently until it holds together.

Lower Calorie

Peppermint Chiffon Pie

Fat and cholesterol are reduced by using whipped dessert topping and eliminating the egg yolks in this light and fluffy peppermint-flavor filling that's mounded into a chocolate cookie crust.

PREP **40 minutes** BAKE **5 minutes** CHILL **15 minutes + 4 to 24 hours** OVEN **at 375°F** MAKES **8 servings**

1 **cup crushed chocolate wafers (16 wafers)**

3 **tablespoons butter, melted**

1 **tablespoon sugar**

3 **cups tiny marshmallows**

2/3 **cup fat-free milk**

1/2 **teaspoon peppermint extract**

4 **drops red food coloring (optional)**

1/4 **cup warm water**

4 **teaspoons dried egg whites**

3 **tablespoons sugar**

1/2 **of an 8-ounce container frozen reduced-fat whipped dessert topping, thawed**

Frozen reduced-fat whipped dessert topping, thawed (optional)

Fresh mint (optional)

1 Preheat oven to 375°F.

2 For crust, in a bowl stir together crushed wafers, melted butter, and 1 tablespoon sugar with a fork. Press mixture onto bottom and up sides of a 9-inch pie plate. Bake for 5 minutes. Cool on a wire rack.

3 For filling, in a medium saucepan combine marshmallows and milk. Cook and stir over medium heat until marshmallows are melted. Remove from heat. Stir in peppermint extract and, if desired, red food coloring. Pour into a large metal bowl. Chill until mixture begins to thicken, stirring occasionally, about 15 to 20 minutes.

4 Remove the peppermint mixture from the refrigerator (it will continue to set). In a medium mixing bowl combine the warm water and dried egg whites. Beat with an electric mixer on medium speed until soft peaks form (tips curl). Gradually add 3 tablespoons sugar, 1 tablespoon at a time, beating on high speed until stiff peaks form (tips stand straight).

5 When peppermint mixture is partially set (consistency of unbeaten egg whites), fold in the egg white mixture. Fold in the whipped topping. If necessary, chill the filling about 30 minutes or until it mounds when spooned.

6 Spoon filling into crust. Cover and chill for 4 to 24 hours or until set. If desired, garnish with additional whipped topping and fresh mint.

NUTRITION FACTS PER SERVING:
233 cal., 8 g total fat (5 g sat. fat), 12 mg chol., 149 mg sodium, 36 g carb., 0 g dietary fiber, 25 g sugar, 2 g protein.

⏱ Apple-Apricot Tartlets

Give apples some unexpected company in the form of apricots and pineapple in these tiny tartlets.

PREP 30 minutes BAKE 10 minutes COOL 5 minutes OVEN at 350°F MAKES 12 servings

²⁄₃ cup quick-cooking rolled oats

½ cup whole wheat flour

¼ cup all-purpose flour

½ of an 8-ounce package reduced-fat cream cheese (Neufchâtel), softened

¼ cup butter, softened

¼ cup packed brown sugar

¼ teaspoon baking soda

¼ teaspoon ground cinnamon

⅛ teaspoon salt

1 medium Granny Smith apple, cored and thinly sliced

2 tablespoons water, apple juice, or apple cider

2 tablespoons low-sugar apricot preserves

4 canned apricot halves, rinsed, drained, and sliced

½ cup fresh or canned pineapple chunks, drained if necessary

1 Preheat oven to 350°F. For pastry, in a small bowl combine oats, whole wheat flour, and all-purpose flour; set aside. In a large bowl beat cream cheese and butter with an electric mixer on medium to high speed for 30 seconds. Add brown sugar, baking soda, cinnamon, and salt; beat until well mixed. Beat in as much of the oat mixture as you can with the mixer. Using a wooden spoon, stir in any remaining oat mixture.

2 Divide pastry into 12 portions; shape into balls. Press balls onto the bottoms and about 1 inch up the sides of twelve 2½-inch muffin cups. Using a fork, prick pastry in several places in each muffin cup.

3 Bake for 10 to 12 minutes or until the edges of the crusts are light brown. Cool in muffin cups on a wire rack for 5 minutes. Remove tart shells from muffin cups; cool completely on a wire rack.

4 For filling, in a small saucepan combine apple and the water. Bring just to boiling; reduce heat. Cover and simmer for 2 to 3 minutes or just until apple slices are softened. Gently stir in preserves. Stir in apricots and pineapple. Spoon fruit mixture into tart shells.

NUTRITION FACTS PER SERVING:
138 cal., 6 g total fat (4 g sat. fat), 17 mg chol., 118 mg sodium, 18 g carb., 2 g dietary fiber, 3 g protein.

Lower Calorie

415

Metric Information

The charts on this page provide a guide for converting measurements from the U.S. customary system, which is used throughout this book, to the metric system.

PRODUCT DIFFERENCES

Most of the ingredients called for in the recipes in this book are available in most countries. However, some are known by different names. Here are some common American ingredients and their possible counterparts:

- All-purpose flour is enriched, bleached, or unbleached white household flour. When self-rising flour is used in place of all-purpose flour in a recipe that calls for leavening, omit the leavening agent (baking soda or baking powder) and salt.
- Baking soda is bicarbonate of soda.
- Cornstarch is cornflour.
- Golden raisins are sultanas.
- Light-color corn syrup is golden syrup.
- Powdered sugar is icing sugar.
- Sugar (white) is granulated, fine granulated, or castor sugar.
- Vanilla or vanilla extract is vanilla essence.

VOLUME AND WEIGHT

The United States traditionally uses cup measures for liquid and solid ingredients. The chart below shows the approximate imperial and metric equivalents. If you are accustomed to weighing solid ingredients, the following approximate equivalents will be helpful.

- 1 cup butter, castor sugar, or rice = 8 ounces = ½ pound = 250 grams
- 1 cup flour = 4 ounces = ¼ pound = 125 grams
- 1 cup icing sugar = 5 ounces = 150 grams

Canadian and U.S. volume for a cup measure is 8 fluid ounces (237 ml), but the standard metric equivalent is 250 ml.

1 British imperial cup is 10 fluid ounces.

In Australia, 1 tablespoon equals 20 ml, and there are 4 teaspoons in the Australian tablespoon.

Spoon measures are used for smaller amounts of ingredients. Although the size of the tablespoon varies slightly in different countries, for practical purposes and for recipes in this book, a straight substitution is all that's necessary. Measurements made using cups or spoons always should be level unless stated otherwise.

COMMON WEIGHT RANGE REPLACEMENTS

Imperial / U.S.	Metric
½ ounce	15 g
1 ounce	25 g or 30 g
4 ounces (¼ pound)	115 g or 125 g
8 ounces (½ pound)	225 g or 250 g
16 ounces (1 pound)	450 g or 500 g
1 ¼ pounds	625 g
1 ½ pounds	750 g
2 pounds or 2 ¼ pounds	1,000 g or 1 Kg

OVEN TEMPERATURE EQUIVALENTS

Fahrenheit Setting	Celsius Setting*	Gas Setting
300°F	150°C	Gas Mark 2 (very low)
325°F	160°C	Gas Mark 3 (low)
350°F	180°C	Gas Mark 4 (moderate)
375°F	190°C	Gas Mark 5 (moderate)
400°F	200°C	Gas Mark 6 (hot)
425°F	220°C	Gas Mark 7 (hot)
450°F	230°C	Gas Mark 8 (very hot)
475°F	240°C	Gas Mark 9 (very hot)
500°F	260°C	Gas Mark 10 (extremely hot)
Broil	Broil	Grill

*Electric and gas ovens may be calibrated using celsius. However, for an electric oven, increase celsius setting 10 to 20 degrees when cooking above 160°C. For convection or forced air ovens (gas or electric), lower the temperature setting 25°F/10°C when cooking at all heat levels.

BAKING PAN SIZES

Imperial / U.S.	Metric
9x1 ½-inch round cake pan	22- or 23x4-cm (1.5 L)
9x1 ½-inch pie plate	22- or 23x4-cm (1 L)
8x8x2-inch square cake pan	20x5-cm (2 L)
9x9x2-inch square cake pan	22- or 23x4.5-cm (2.5 L)
11x7x1 ½-inch baking pan	28x17x4-cm (2 L)
2-quart rectangular baking pan	30x19x4.5-cm (3 L)
13x9x2-inch baking pan	34x22x4.5-cm (3.5 L)
15x10x1-inch jelly roll pan	40x25x2-cm
9x5x3-inch loaf pan	23x13x8-cm (2 L)
2-quart casserole	2 L

U.S./STANDARD METRIC EQUIVALENTS

⅛ teaspoon = 0.5 ml	
¼ teaspoon = 1 ml	
½ teaspoon = 2 ml	
1 teaspoon = 5 ml	
1 tablespoon = 15 ml	
2 tablespoons = 25 ml	
¼ cup = 2 fluid ounces = 50 ml	
⅓ cup = 3 fluid ounces = 75 ml	
½ cup = 4 fluid ounces = 125 ml	
⅔ cup = 5 fluid ounces = 150 ml	
¾ cup = 6 fluid ounces = 175 ml	
1 cup = 8 fluid ounces = 250 ml	
2 cups = 1 pint = 500 ml	
1 quart = 1 litre	